BE COMFORTABLE
WITH FRIENDS

RONALD M. GIFFORD

authorHOUSE®

AuthorHouse™
1663 Liberty Drive
Bloomington, IN 47403
www.authorhouse.com
Phone: 1-800-839-8640

Published by AuthorHouse   03/04/2015

ISBN: 978-1-4969-3467-3 (sc)
ISBN: 978-1-4969-3466-6 (e)

Library of Congress Control Number: 2014914912

Print information available on the last page.

CONTENTS

FOREWORD

THERE IS ONE STORY IN THIS BOOK THAT IS FICTIONAL, THE REST ARE ALL WRITTEN ABOUT EVENTS THAT REALLY HAPPENED. MOST OF THE STORIES ARE FROM HAPPENINGS IN MY OWN PERSONAL LIFE, SOME FROM STORIES I'VE HEARD, AND ONE FROM HISTORY OF EARLY AMERICA. SOME OF THE NAMES OF PERSONS IN THE STORIES HAVE BEEN CHANGED AND THE DIALOGUE IS NOT VERBATIM, BUT IS AS CLOSE TO BEING RIGHT AS I CAN REMEMBER. THE STORIES STRETCH OUT OVER A LONG PERIOD OF TIME FROM THE EARLY 1600s INTO THE 1980s.

RONALD M. GIFFORD

INTRODUCTION

IF YOU HAVE READ MY POETRY BOOK, 'TAKE TIME FOR A STROLL', OR WILL READ A FEW OF THE STORIES IN THIS BOOK, YOU'LL KNOW ME BECAUSE I WRITE AND TALK JUST LIKE I THINK. YOU WON'T HAVE TO LOOK ANY WORDS FROM THIS BOOK UP IN THE DICTIONARY TO FIGURE OUT MY MEANING. WHEN I WAS VERY YOUNG, THROUGH TRIAL AND ERROR, I FOUND THAT KEEPING THINGS SIMPLE AND HONEST WAS THE EASIEST AND BEST WAY FOR ME TO DO THINGS AND IT'S WORKED FOR ME IN MANY WAYS THROUGHOUT MY LIFE.

MOST PEOPLE AREN'T WHO THEY LOOK LIKE, THE INNER-PERSON IS THE MOST IMPORTANT PART OF MOST PEOPLE, WORK ON IT AND YOU'LL SUCCEED IN LIFE WITH LIFE. WISDOM AND NATURAL TALENT CAN NEITHER BE LEARNED NOR TAUGHT. THEY ARE A SPECIAL GIFT, CHERISH AND NURTURE THEM. KEEP THINGS SIMPLE AND BE HONEST AND TRUTHFUL TO YOURSELF IN EVERY WAY... RONALD M. GIFFORD

AN INTRODUCTION TO YESTERDAY

THE CHILDREN BORN AND RAISED DURING THE NINETEEN TWENTIES, THIRTIES AND FORTIES AND I WAS ONE OF THEM, HAD A HUGE ADVANTAGE OVER THE CHILDREN THAT CAME ALONG LATER. WE DIDN'T HAVE MUCH IN MATERIAL THINGS THAT WAS NORMAL FOR EVERYONE AT THE TIME IN MY NEIGHBORHOOD. OUR EXPECTATIONS WEREN'T VERY HIGH. BUT WE DID HAVE HOPES AND DREAMS. IT WAS GOOD JUST TO BE ALIVE AND HAVE FRIENDS.

I GREW UP ON THE SOUTHWEST SIDE OF CHICAGO IN A WORKING CLASS NEIGHBORHOOD. PEOPLE TRIED TO LIVE AS CLOSE TO THEIR WORK PLACE AS POSSIBLE SO THEY COULD WALK TO WORK. THERE WERE VERY FEW AUTOMOBILES IN OUR AREA AT THE TIME.

A BOTTLE OF POP, A CANDY BAR, AN ICE CREAM CONE, A CUP OF COFFEE AND A DOUGHNUT WERE ALL FIVE CENTS APIECE. PENNY CANDY WAS VERY POPULAR AT THE TIME. A HAMBURGER OR A TRIP TO THE MOVIES COST A DIME AND WE COULDN'T AFFORD ANY OF THEM MOST OF THE TIME. THE HARD TIMES DIDN'T REALLY

BOTHER US KIDS, WE WEREN'T AWARE OF THE STRESS AND HARDSHIPS THAT OUR PARENTS WERE GOING THROUGH, THEY ACTED AS THOUGH EVERYTHING WAS FINE AND NORMAL.

I BROWN BAGGED IT THROUGH GRADE SCHOOL AND HIGH SCHOOL AND NEVER FELT DEPRIVED OF ANYTHING. I LIKE HARD BOILED EGGS, PEANUT BUTTER AND JELLY OR BALONEY SANDWICHES, A PIECE OF FRUIT AND SOME HOMEMADE COOKIES OR CAKE AND I STILL DO.

MOST KIDS OF THE NEIGHBORHOOD GOT ALONG FINE TOGETHER. SMALL GIRLS PLAYED HOUSE, CUT OUT PAPER DOLLS AND HAD TEA PARTIES. OTHERS PLAYED JACKS, HOP SCOTCH AND JUMPED ROPE. MOST KIDS ENJOYED SIDEWALK ROLLER SKATING. BOYS SPUN TOPS, FLEW KITES, SHOT MARBLES AND PLAYED COPS AND ROBBERS, COWBOYS AND INDIANS AND ALL KINDS OF SPORTS. EVERYONE PLAYED TAG, HIDE AND SEEK AND A LOT OF OTHER GAMES AND THINGS THAT KIDS COULD DO TOGETHER. NOT MUCH EQUIPMENT REQUIRED AND NO ADULTS INVOLVED. WE MADE FIRENDSHIPS AT AN EARLY AGE, BOTH MALE AND FEMALE THAT HAVE LASTED A LIFETIME.

I WOULDN'T TRADE MY CHILDHOOD AND GROWING UP DURING THE DEPRESSION WITH ANY OTHER TIME PERIOD THAT I CAN THINK OF. WE LEARNED VALUES, NOT ONLY ABOUT MONEY. WE LEARNED THE VALUE OF HONEST, INTEGRITY, LOYALITY, ATTITUDE AND A GOOD

SENSE OF HUMOR. BEING ABLE TO LAUGH AT OURSELVES AND EACH OTHER WITHOUT ANY USE OF MALICE.

LIFE IS SWEET, IT JUST DEPENDS ON HOW YOU LOOK AT IT AND USE IT. WE LEARNED RESPECT, NOT ONLY FOR OUR ELDERS, BUT FOR EVERYONE. NO MATTER HOW RICH OR POOR WE MAY BE, WE'RE ALL JUST HUMAN BEINGS. WE ALL HAVE FEELINGS AND THERE IS NO PURPOSE SERVED, TRAMPLING ON ANOTHER PERSONS FEELINGS.

BACK THEN, MEN AND BOYS TIPPED THEIR HATS, OPENED DOORS AND GAVE UP THEIR SEATS TO LADIES AND THE ELDERLY.

IT WAS A MUCH KINDER AND GENTLER TIME......

AN APRIL MORNING IN CHICAGO

MOM SHOOK ME AWAKE AND SAID, COME ON BUD, IT'S TIME TO GET UP AND HAVE YOUR BREAKFAST.

I GOT DRESSED AND WENT OUT TO THE KITCHEN WHERE DAD WAS SITTING AT THE TABLE EATING OATMEAL, CANTALOPE AND TOAST.

HE LOOKED AT ME AND SAID, SIT DOWN AND EAT SON, WE'RE GOING OVER TO THE AIRPORT IN A LITTLE WHILE AND LOOK AT AN AIRPLANE. I LIKED AIRPLANES, AND BEING UP CLOSE TO ONE WAS EVEN BETTER. WE DIDN'T HAVE A CAR SO WHEN WE GOT OUTSIDE OUR HOUSE, DAD LIFTED ME UP ONTO HIS SHOURLDRS AND WALKED THE THREE BLOCKS TO THE AIRPORT LIKE THAT.

WHEN WE GOT TO THE AIRPORT, DAD WALKED TWO MORE BLOCKS UP THE STREET TO WHERE A LARGE CROWD OF PEOPLE HAD GATHERED BETWEEN TWO AIRPLANE HANGERS.

THERE WAS A CHAINLINK FENCE A WAYS IN OFF THE STREET SO THAT PEOPLE COULD GO IN THERE AND

WATCH PLANES, BUT THEY COULDN'T GO ALL THE WAY TO THE RUNWAYS.

THE CROWD WAS JUST STANDING THERE QUIETLY LOOKING OUT AT THE RUNWAY. I WAS STILL SITTING ON DADS SHOULDERS AND DIDN'T KNOW WHAT WE WERE LOOKING FOR.

IN A SHORT WHILE A SMALL SILVER PLANE APPEARED ON THE RUNWAY AND TURNED TOWARD US BETWEEN THE TWO HANGERS.

THE PLANE STOPPED AND I COULD SEE THE HEAD OF A PERSON THROUGH THE PLANES FRONT WINDOW.

THE RUNWAYS IN THOSE DAYS WEREN'T MADE OF CEMENT OR ASPHALT; THEY WERE MADE OF CINDERS AND ASHES FROM BURNT COAL.

THE PLANE BEGAN TO MOVE AGAIN AND IT WAS HEADED RIGHT TOWARD US. THE CROWD BEGAN TO CHEER AND WHISTLE AND WAVE THEIR ARMS. THE PILOT IN THE PLANE WAVED BACK.

THE PLANE CAME ALMOST UP TO THE FENCE AND THEN BEGAN TO TURN AROUND. THE BACKWASH FROM THE PROPELLER SENT A CLOUD OF DUST AND CINDERS INTO THE AIR THAT COVERED THE CROWD OF PEOPLE. THEY WERE NO LONGER CHEERING. THEY WERE RUNNING THIS WAY AND THAT TRYING TO GET OUT OF THE DUST

CLOUD. WHEN DAD AND I GOT HOME, WE BOTH TOOK LONG BATHS.

YEARS LATER WHEN MY HISTORY TEACHER AT SCHOOL TOLD OUR CLASS ABOUT THE VERY FIRST SOLO FLIGHT FROM AMERICA TO EUROPE MADE BY CHARLES A. LINDBERGH AND HOW IMPORTANT IT WAS, I REMEMBERED THAT MORNING IN APRIL, 1927 WHEN THAT LITTLE SILVER PLANE HAD STOPPED IN CHICAGO TO REFUEL ON ITS WAY TO NEW YORK......

SNOW MADE THE DIFFERENCE

WHEN THE HOLIDAY SEASON APPROACHES, PICTURES OF A LONG AGO CHRISTMAS EVE CAME VIVIDLY BACK TO ME. IT WAS 1932 IN CHICAGO AND I WAS NINE YEARS OLD. THE TIME WAS ABOUT EIGHT O'CLOCK IN THE EVENING AND IT WAS VERY COLD OUTSIDE. I MADE A ROUND HOLE IN THE FROST IN OUR FRONT ROOM WINDOW WITH MY FINGER TIPS. LOOKING THROUGH THE HOLE I COULD SEE THAT THE ONLY MOVEMENT OUTSIDE WAS THAT OF LARGE SNOWFLAKES AS THEY GENTLY FLOATED DOWN AND QUICKLY COVERED THE GROUND. LONG ICE-CYCLES HUNG FROM THE EAVES OF EVERY HOUSE THAT I COULD SEE, SMOKE CURLING FROM EVERY CHIMNEY. I STARED HARD THROUGH THE HOLE AND IMAGINED THAT OUR SMALL BUNEGLOW ON THE SOUTHWEST SIDE OF THE CITY HAD BECOME A COZY COTTAGE, SITTING IN THE MIDDLE OF A WOODED AREA WITH A BRIGHTLY BURNING FIRE IN A STONE FIREPLACE. THE SMELL OF THE SMOKE THAT DRIFTED OUT OF OUR CHINMEY BLENDED WITH THE AROMA OF THE FIR TREES ON THE GROUND AND CLUNG TO THE TREE BRANCED AND BUSHES HAD TRANSFORMED MY NEIGHBORHOOD INTO A CLEAN PRISTINE PLACE THAT WILL ALWAYS BE IN MY MEMORIES......

I WAS TO PASS ANOTHER MILE-STONE THAT YEAR, IN NOVEMBER I'D TURN 10 YEARS OLD. IT WOULDN'T BE JUST ANOTHER BIRTHDAY; I'D BE OLD ENOUGH TO GET A PAPER ROUTE. THE TROUBLE WAS THAT I DIDN'T OWN A BICYCLE. HAVING A BIKE AND BEING TEN YEARS OLD WERE THE TWO REQUIREMENTS NEEDED TO GET A NEWSPAPER DELIVERY JOB. YOU COULD MAKE FROM FIFTY CENTS TO TWO DOLLARS A WEEK DEPENDING ON HOW MANY CUSTOMERS YOU HAD AND THAT WAS GOOD MONEY TO A KID IN 1933.

I HAD BEEN DELIVERING LIBERTY MAGAZINES FOR A YEAR OR SO. LIBERTY MAGAZINE CAME OUT WEEKLY AND COST FIVE CENTS. I MADE A PENNY ON EACH ONE I DELIVERED AND I HAD NINE CUSTOMERS. IT MADE ME DIZZY TO THINK OF WHAT I COULD DO WITH PAPER ROUTE MONEY.

I NEEDED TO GET A DEPENDABLE USED BIKE. I HAD FOUR DOLLARS AND EIGHTY SIX CENTS IN MY SOX AND HANKERCHIEF DRAWER AND DOUBTED THAT IT WOULD BE ENOUGH TO BUY A DECENT BIKE FOR THAT.

I COULD PROBABLY BUY A BEAT UP ONE AND SEE IF MY COUSIN JOHNNY WOULD HELP ME FIX IT UP. JOHNNY WAS ALWAYS WORKING ON HIS BIKE AND OTHER PEOPLES TOO, HE KNEW ALL ABOUT THEM.

IT WAS MID-JULY AND HOT. I HAD JUST FINISHED MOWING THE GRASS IN THE BACK YARD WHEN JOHNNY

SHOWED UP AND SAID, I HEARD YOU WANT TO TALK TO ME I ANSWERED YES AND WE WALKED OVER TO THE BACK PORCH AND SAT ON THE STEPS IN THE SHADE.

I TOLD HIM WHAT MY PROBLEM WAS AND ASKED IF HE COULD HELP ME FIND A USED BIKE AND FIX IT UP. I TOLD HIM THAT I ONLY HAD FOUR DOLLARS. I WAS HOLDING BACK ON THE EIGHTY SIX CENTS. I DIDN'T WANT TO BE TOTALLY BROKE.

JOHNNY SAT THER A LONG TIME, LOOKING STRAIGHT AHEAD. THEN HE SAID, I CAN SCOUT AROUND AND COME UP WITH SOMETHING FOR YOU. THERE'S SOMETHING ELSE WE CAN TRY, IT'S A LONG SHOT. THERE'S A BOY IN MY CLASS WHOSE FAMILY IS MOVING TO NEW YORK AND HE CAN'T TAKE HIS BIKE WITH HIM. HE'S BEEN TRYING TO SELL IT FOR THE LAST COUPLE OF WEEKS WITH NO LUCK. I THINK THE BIKE'S PRETTY NEW AND WORTH A LOT MORE THEN FOUR DOLLARS, BUT THEY CAN'T SHOOT US FOR TRYING. GET YOUR MONEY AND WE'LL SEE IF TOMS HOME. JOHNNY AND I WALKED ABOUT THREE BLOCKS OR SO OVER TO PARKSIDE AVENEUE TO A LARGE APARTMENT BUILDING AND WENT AROUND TO THE BACK, AND JOHNNY TOLD ME TO WAIT IN THE COURTYARD. HE CLIMBED SOME STAIRS UP TO THE SECOND FLOOR, WALKD DOWN A WAYS AND KNOCKED ON A DOOR AND WAITED.

IN A LITTLE WHILE A BOY CAME OUT. THEY TALKED AND THEN CAME DOWN AND JOINED ME.

TOM THE BOY SAID HI TO ME AND WENT DOWN SOME STEPS AND INTO THE BASEMENT. HE CAME BACK OUT RIGHT AWAY WHEELING A BEAUTIFUL MAROON BICYCLE. IT LOOKED NEW. IT WAS A RANGER AND HAD A BIG BASKET ON THE FRONT AND HAD BALLOON TIRES, IT WAS PERFECT. NOT IN MY WILDEST DREAMS COULD I EVER HAVE IMAGINED OWNING SUCH A BIKE, AND SURELY NOT FOR ANY FOUR DOLLARS.

TOM ASKED ME IF I WANTED TO TRY IT OUT.

I DECLINED AND EXPLAINED THAT I DIDN'T KNOW HOW TO RIDE YET. JOHNNY GRABBED AHOLD OF THE HANDLE BARS AND JUMPED A-STRADDLE ONTO THE SEAT, LIKE A COWBOY LEAPING INTO HIS SADDLE AND HOLLERED, I'LL TEST IT OUR FOR YOU AS HE RACED OFF AROUND THE BUILDING.

TOM AND I DIDN'T SAY ANYTHING TO EACH OTHER WHILE JOHNNY WAS GONE. I WAS NATURALLY SHY AND I FIGURED THAT TOM WAS FEELING BAD BECAUSE HE HAD TO SELL HIS BEAUTIFUL BIKE.

PRETTY SOON JOHNNY CAME PEDDLING AROUND THE CORNER OF THE BUILDING FAST AND MADE A SKIDDING SIDEWAYS STOP RIGHT IN FRONT OF US AND SAID THAT EVERYTHING ABOUT THE BIKE WAS OK.

HE WAS GOING TO TALK WITH TOM FOR A LITTLE WHILE.

I WALKED TO THE FRONT OF THE BUILDING AND SAT DOWN ON THE CURB. I WAS SURE THAT I WASN'T GOING TO GET THAT BICYCLE. NOT FOR ANY FOUR DOLLARS.

IN ALMOST NO TIME AT ALL, JOHNNY ALMOST RAN OVER ME WITH THE BIKE AND SAID, HERE TAKE YOUR BIKE AND GIVE ME THREE DOLLARS. I'LL BE RIGHT BACK AND WE'LL TAKE YOUR NEW BIKE HOME AND TOMORROW I'LL TEACH YOU HOW TO RIDE IT.

WE WALKED THE BIKE TO MY HOUSE AND ON THE WAY JOHNNY TOLD ME ABOUT HIS SHORT TALK WITH TOM. THE MOVING VAN WAS COMING EARLY IN THE MORNING TO LOAD UP THEIR FURNITURE AND THEN TOMS FAMILY WAS TAKING THE TRAIN TO NEW YORK. TOM HADN'T BEEN ABLE TO SELL HIS BIKE SO HE WAS JUST GOING TO LEAVE IT IN THE BASEMENT. JOHNNY SAID THAT HE OFFERED TOM THREE DOLLARS, FIGURING TO USE THE FORTH ONE TO HAGGLE WITH BUT TOM DIDN'T TRY TO HAGGLE, HE TOOK THE THREE DOLLARS AND SAID GOOD BY TO JOHNNY.

AFTER JOHNNY LEFT MY PLACE I PUT THE BIKE UNDER THE BACK PORCH AND LOOKED AT IT IN DISBELIEF. I TRIED TO THINK OF HOW I WOULD TELL MY FOLKS WHAT HAD JUST HAPPENED. IT ALL HAPPENED SO FAST THAT MY HEAD WAS SPINNING; IT WAS HARD TO THINK PAST MY BEAUTIFUL NEW BIKE. DID IT REALLY HAPPEN? WAS IT REALLY MINE? ABOUT HALF WAY THROUGH SUPPER I COULDN'T HOLD MY EXCITEMENT ANY LONGER, I WAS

HAVING TROUBLE TRYING TO EAT SO I BLURTED OUT TO THE ROOM, IN A HIGHER PITCH THAN NORMAL VOICE, I BOUGHT SOMETHING TODAY.

MY MOTHER, FATHER AND SISTER KEPT ON EATING AND DIDN'T SEEM INTERESTED IN WHAT I JUST SAID.

MY SISTER FINALLY LOOKED AT ME AND ASKED, WHAT'D YOU BUY, I BET IT WAS A NEW TOP OR SOME MARBLES.

NOBODY SHOWED ANY INTEREST SO I SAID, IT'S A LOT BIGGER.

THEY ALL STOPPED EATING AND LOOKED AT ME AND MOM ASKED, WHAT IS IT BUD, WHAT DID YOU BUY?

I ANSWERED; IT'S IN THE BACK YARD, UNDER THE PORCH.

ALL OF A SUDDEN THE REST OF SUPPER COULD WAIT. MY SISTER SAID, COME ON THEN AND SHOW US. WE ALL WENT OUT TO THE BACK YARD AND I WENT UNDER THE PORCH AND CAME OUT WHEELING THE BIKE. EVERYBODY STOOD THERE, NOT WITH THEIR MOUTHS OPENED BUT THEIR EYES WERE SURE WIDE OPENED.

MOM ASKED, WHERE DID IT COME FROM? IT'S SURE PRETTY.

DAD ASKED, WHERE DID YOU GET THE MONEY FOR SUCH A BIKE?

I TOLD THEM THE WHOLE STORY OF HOW I CAME TO GET IT.

MY SISTER SAID, YOU DON'T EVEN KNOW HOW TO RIDE A BIKE.

I ANSWERED WITH, I CAN LEARN. I FIGURED THAT DAD WOULD BE BUYING ANOTHER BIKE, SOON.

DAD PATTED ME ON THE BACK AND SAID THAT I HAD MADE A VERY GOOD DEAL.

WHAT HE SAID KINDA PUFFED ME UP. BUT I KNEW THAT WITHOUT JOHNNYS GREAT HELP, IT NEVER WOULD HAVE HAPPENED AND I ALSO KNEW THAT I WAS ABOUT THE LUCKIEST KID IN CHICAGO THAT DAY. JOHNNY CAME OVER THE NEXT DAY AND STARTED TEACHING ME ALL KINDS OF THINGS ABOUT A BIKE. AFTER HE TOLD ME A FEW THINGS HE'D ASK ME QUESTIONS ABOUT WHAT HE HAD JUST TOLD ME. I DIDN'T KNOW THERE WAS SO MUCH TO LEARN ABOUT A BIKE BEFORE YOU COULD RIDE ONE. I THOUGHT THAT YOU JUST GOT ON AND STARTED PEDDLING. NEXT HE TOLD ME ABOUT THE LAWS FOR RIDING A BIKE IN THE STREET, JUST LIKE DRIVERS OF CARS YOU HAVE TO KNOW. AND OBEY THEM.

JOHNNY WAS KINDA TOUGH AND WOULN'T LET UP ON ME. HE SAID, I'M GOING TO ASK YOU ALL THIS STUFF TOMORROW AND WHEN YOU KNOW IT GOOD WE'LL GET ON WITH THE RIDING PART.

JOHNNY WAS TRUE TO HIS WORD. AS SOON AS HE WAS SATISFIED THAT I KNEW WHAT HE HAD TAUGHT ME, HE SHOWED ME HOW TO GET ON AND OFF THE BIKE AND HAD ME PEDDLING DOWN THE STREET WITH HIM RUNNING ALONG SIDE WITH HIS HANDS ON THE BACK OF THE SEAT AND THE BACK FENDER. WHEN HE FINALLY LET GO AND SAID KEEP PEDDLING, YOU'RE ON YOUR OWN. I WASN'T GOING VERY FAST AND I FELT KINDA SHAKY. RIDING THE BIKE GAVE ME A FEELING OF FREEDOM, WITH THE WIND IN MY FACE AND THINGS GOING BY PRETTY FAST. IT SURE BEAT WALKING. I REALLY LIKE THE FEELING.

AFTER A WEEK OF PRACTICE RIDING I WENT OVER TO THE NEWS AGENCY AND TOLD THE AGENT THAT I'D BE TEN IN NOVEMBER AND WOULD LIKE TO APPLY FOR A JOB. HE GAVE ME A CARD TO FILL OUT AND TOLD ME HE'D LET ME KNOW WHEN A ROUTE OPENED UP. I FIGURED THAT A LOT OF KIDS WANTED JOBS TOO SO I'D PROBABLY HAVE A LONG WAIT BEFORE ONE CAME UP FOR ME.

SCHOOL ALWAYS STARTED RIGHT AFTER LABOR DAY. IT DIDN'T SEEM RIGHT TO ME. THE WEATHER WAS STILL HOT AND THE CLASS ROOMS WERE STUFFY. A GUY HAD A HARD TIME THINKING ABOUT LEARNING AND DOING HOME WORK IN SUCH NICE WEATHER. SCHOOL SHOULD BE WHEN THE WEATHER'S BAD AND THERE'S NOTHING ELSE TO THINK ABOUT. ABOUT TWO WEEKS BEFORE SCHOOL WAS TO START I GOT A PHONE CALL FROM THE NEWSPAPER AGENT, MR. MAC. IT WAS ABOUT TWO

THIRTY IN THE AFTERNOON. SIS WAS OUT SOMEPLACE AND MOM AND DAD WEREN'T HOME FROM WORK YET. MR. MAC WANTED TO KNOW IF I COULD COME TO WORK TODAY, RIGHT NOW. I WAS KINDA STUNNED AND DIDN'T KNOW WHAT TO SAY. MY MOUTH MADE UP MY MIND FOR ME WHEN IT SAID YES. I'LL BE RIGHT OVER. I LEFT MOM A NOTE AND PEDDLED OVER TO THE AGENCY.

MR. MAC EXPLAINED TO ME THAT THE REGULAR PAPERBOY HAD QUIT TWO DAYS BEFORE AND THAT HE, MR. MAC HAD BEEN DELIVERING THE PAPERS IN HIS CAR. NOBODY ELSE WANTED THE ROUTE SO HE WAS GIVING IT TO ME. I FOUND OUT PRETTY QUICK WHY NOBODY WANTED IT. THE ROUTE WAS THE WORST ONE IN TOWN. IT WENT WAY OUT INTO THE BOON-DOCKS AND WAS REALLY SPREAD OUT. THERE WERE ONLY FORTY SEVEN COUSTOMERS BUT IT TOOK LONGER THEN ANY OTHER ROUTE TO FINISH.

MR. MAC SHOWED ME HOW TO FOLD THE PAPER TOGETHER. THEY HAD TO BE FOLDED RIGHT SO THEY WOULD HOLD TOGETHER WHEN YOU THREW THEM UP ON THE PORCHES OR IN FRONT OF DOORS. IF YOU HAD TO GET OFF YOUR BIKE AND LAY THEM BY THE DOORS, YOU'D NEVER GET DONE. WE DIDN'T USE RUBBER BANDS TO HOLD THEM TOGETHER BACK THEN.

MR. MAC GAVE ME A BRAND NEW CANVAS BAG AND HELPED ME FILL IT WITH PAPERS. I PUT THE BAG INTO THE BASKET AND HE SHOWED ME HOW TO WRAP

THE SHOULDER STRAPS OF THE BAG AROUND THE HANDLEBARS OF MY BIKE SO THE BAG WOULDN'T BOUNCE OUT WHEN I HIT BUMPS. NEXT HE SHOWED ME WHERE MY ROUTE WAS ON A BIG MAP HANGING ON THE WALL OF HIS OFFICE. HE GAVE ME A LARGE METAL RING WITH A BUNCH OF YELLOW CARDS ON IT AND TOLD ME TO SLIP IT ONTO MY HANDLEBARS. HE EXPLAINED THAT THE FIRST CARD WAS MY FIRST CUSTOMER AND SO ON, AND HE ADDED, DON'T LOSE THEM. AS I RODE OFF IN A DAZE, MR. MAC SAID, IT SHOULD TAKE YOU ABOUT TWO HOURS. I'LL SEE YOU TOMORROW.

THAT FIRST DAY IT TOOK ME OVER THREE HOURS TO DO THE ROUTE. BY THE TIME I GOT HOME IT WAS ALMOST SIX O'CLOCK. MOM HAD KEPT MY SUPPER WARM FOR ME BUT I COULD TELL THAT SHE WASN'T HAPPY ABOUT ME GETTING HOME SO LATE.

MY ROUTE RAN WAY OUT PAST THE COMMUNITIES EDGE. SOME STREETS HAD ONLY THREE OR FOUR HOUSES ON THE WHOLE BLOCK. I WAS ZIG ZAGGING BACK AND FORTH AND SOME OF THE HOUSES DIDN'T HAVE ANY NUMBERS ON THEM, I HAD TO GUESS BECAUSE ACCORDING TO THE YELLOW CARDS I WAS ON THE RIGHT STREET. MY LAST FEW CUSTOMERS LIVED OUT PAST THE PAVED ROADS AND SIDEWALKS, THERE WAS JUST A DIRT PATH TO FOLLOW AND THERE WERE NO STREET LIGHTS.

BEFORE I LEFT THE NEWS AGENCY, MR. MAC HANDED ME ANOTHER PAPER AND EXPLAINED THAT I'D ALWAYS

GET AN EXTRA PAPER EVERY DAY, JUST IN CASE. HE DIDN'T SAY IN CASE WHAT. SO I TOOK A PAPER HOME ALMOST EVERY NIGHT. AT THE END OF THE FIRST DAY I STILL HAD THREE PAPERS IN MY BAG WHEN I GOT THROUGH, WHICH MEANT THAT I HAD MISSED TWO HOUSES. I WENT OVER AND OVER MY CUSTOMER LIST THAT NIGHT AND COULDN'T FIGURE OUT WHO I HAD SKIPPEDD. FRIDAY WAS COLLECTION DAY AND I'D HAVE TO ASK EACH OF MY CUSTOMERS IF I HAD MISSED THEM.

I HAD FORTY SEVEN CUSTOMERS, AT TWO CENTS EACH PER WEEK I'D MAKE NINETY FOUR CENTS, NOT BAD. THE TROUBLE WAS THAT THE VERY FIRST DAY, I THREW A PAPER THROUGH A WINDOW. THE BROKEN WINDOW COST ME A DOLLAR AND TWENTY CENTS TO REPLACE, SO THE FIRST WEEK I LOST TWENTY SIX CENTS.

I FIGURED MAYBE MY FIRST WORKING DAY MIGHT BE MY LAST. THE SECOND DAY I WENT IN AN HOUR EARLY, THE PAPERS WEREN'T THERE YET AND NEITHER WERE THE OTHER PAPERBOYS. I WANTED TO EXPLAIN TO MR. MAC WHAT HAD HAPPENED THAT FIRST DAY. I DIDN'T WANT THE OTHER KIDS LISTENING TO MY STORY. WHEN I WAS THROUGH TELLING MR. MAC WHAT HAD HAPPENED, HE LOOKED A ME AND KINDA LAUGHED AND SAID, I THINK YOU'LL DO ALRIGHT HERE; YOU DIDN'T TRY TO LIE TO ME. WE'LL GET YOU STRAIGHTENED OUT.

DURING THE NEXT FEW WEEKS I CHANGED MY ROUTE AROUND SOME AND FIGURED OUT HOW I COULD GET

MY DELIVERY TIME DOWN. SOME BLOCKS I'D WORK JUST ONE END OF THE STREET GOING OUT, AND AFTER DOING WHAT HAD BEEN THE ORGINAL END OF THE ROUTE, I'D DELIVER THE OTHER END OF THE SPARSE BLOCKS COMING BACK. I COULD USUALLY FINISH AND BE HOME BEFORE FIVE THIRTY. MOM SAID IT WAS ALRIGHT AS LONG AS I KEPT MY GRADES AT SCHOOL UP. I HAD NEVER GOTTEN BETTER THEN AVERAGE GRADES, SO I FIGURED I HAD TO BUCKLE DOWN NOW.

BEING AT SCHOOL ALL DAY, THEN THE PAPER ROUTE, HOME WORK AND STUDYING, I DIDN'T HAVE ANY TIME FOR PLAYING EXCEPT ON THE WEEK ENDS. MY GRADES ACTUALLY IMPROVED IN SOME SUBJECTS. I GUESS THE PAPER JOB WAS AN INCENTIVE FOR ME TO TRY HARDER. I HAD PICKED UP TWO NEW CUSTOMERS, AND SOME PEOPLE WOULD GIVE ME AN EXTRA PENNY OR TWO ON COLLECTION DAY SO I WAS MAKING A DOLLAR A WEEK OR SO.

ON SATURDAYS I HAD THE CHORE OF SCRUBBING THE INSIDE BASEMENT STAIRS AND ALSO DOING THE FRONT PROCH AND STEPS. IN BAD WETHER I JUST SWEPT THE PROCH AND STEPS. MY SISTERS JOB WAS TO SCRUB THE BATHROOM AND KITCHEN FLOORS AND SINKS. WE KNEW THAT WE HAD TO DO THESE JOBS SO WE GOT RIGHT TO THEM ON SATURDAY MORNINGS. AFTER LUNCH I HAD PLENTY OF TIME FOR THE MOVIES AND HANGING OUT WITH MY FRIENDS.

THE CHRISTMAS AND EASTER BREAKS TOOK ON A SPECIAL MEANING FOR ME. MOST OF MY CUSTOMERS GAVE ME A LITTLE EXTRA MONEY AT CHRISTMAS TIME AND WE GOT A WEEK OFF FROM SCHOOL FOR EACH HOLIDAY. THERE WERE TIMES TO LOOK FORWARD TO. I GUESS IT WOULD BE THE SAME FOR GROWNUPS WHEN THEY GOT SOME TIME OFF FOR VACATIONS AFTER WORKING ALL YEAR. I COULD PLAY BASEBALL AND HANG OUT WITH MY BUDDIES ALL SUMMER, THAT WAS SOMETHING TO REALLY THINK ABOUT.

MY DAYS WENT RIGHT ALONG, I GUESS I HAD GOTTEN INTO A ROUTINE. THE FIRST SNOW OF WINTER CHANGED EVERYTHING.

WHEN I GOT TO THE NEWS AGENCY THAT DAY I NOTICED THAT MOST OF THE OTHER KIDS HAD BROUGHT WAGONS INSTEAD OF BICYCLES. ONE OF THE BOYS EXPLAINED THAT IT WAS A LOT EASIER PULLING A WAGON IN THE SNOW THEN TRYING TO RIDE A BIKE THROUGH IT.

I SOON FOUND OUT WHAT HE MEANT AFTER I SLID AND FELL A COUPLE OF TIMES AND MY PAPERS WERE SCATTERED AROUND ON THE WET SNOW. I STRUGGLED A LOT THAT DAY JUST TO GET DONE. I WAS VERY LATE GETTING HOME AND KNEW I'D BE LATER THEN USUAL IF THE SNOW KEPT PILING UP. THAT NIGHT I PUT A WOODEN BOX IN MY WAGON AND COVERED IT WITH AN OLD PIECE OF CANVAS. I MIGHT GET WET, THAT WAS OK, BUT MY PAPERS WOULDN'T.

PULLING THE WAGON WORKED OUT FINE, AND LATER WHEN THE SNOW HAD REALLY PILED UP, ALL THE PAPERBOYS SWITCHED TO SLEDS. ON THE WAGON AND SLED DAYS I DIDN'T GET HOME UNTIL SIX O'CLOCK OR LATER. WITH THE SHORTER DAYS OF WINTER IT WAS USUALLY DARK BY THE TIME I GOT HOME. MOM SEEMED TO UNDERSTAND, BECAUSE SHE NEVER MENTIONED IT TO ME.

1933 WAS THE FIRST YEAR THAT I BOUGHT CHRISTMAS PRESENTS FOR MY MOM, DAD AND SISTER, IT MADE ME FEEL GOOD TO DO SO. I ALSO BOUGHT MYSELF A NEW PAIR OF ICESKATES. THEY WERE SHOE SKATES. BEFORE THAT, I HAD CLAMP-ON SKATES THAT CLAMPED ONTO MY REGULAR SHOES, LIKE ROLLER SKATES DID AT THAT TIME.

BUYING THE BIKE WAS A BETTER INVESTMENT THAN ANY OF US COULD HAVE EVER IMAGINED. A GREAT INVESTMENT.

AFTER CHRISTMAS I DIDN'T HAVE THE TIME OR THE WANT TO SPEND MUCH MONEY, SO IT KEPT MOUNTING UP IN MY SOX DRAWER. MY SISTER CALLED ME A MISER WHICH DIDN'T BOTHER ME A BIT.

A COUPLE OF WEEKS AFTER CHRISTMAS I ASKED MOM IF KIDS COULD PUT MONEY IN THE SAVINGS BANK DOWN TOWN.

SHE ANSWERED, I DON'T KNOW BUT WE CAN FIND OUT NEXT SATURDAY MORNING IF YOU WANT TO.

SATURDAY MOM AND I WALKED DOWN TO THE BANK AND TALKED TO THE BANK PRESIDENT. IT WAS A SMALL BANK WITH TWO TELLERS, A SECRETARY AND THE PRESIDENT. MOM ASKED HIM IF I COULD OPEN AN ACCOUNT. HE TOLD US THAT HE'D BE HAPPY TO HAVE ME AS A NEW CUSTOMER WITH MOM AS CO-SIGNER. I COULD DEPOSIT MONEY, A DOLLAR OR MORE AT A TIME BUT MOM WOULD HAVE TO MAKE THE WITHDRAWALS. THAT SOUNDED GOOD TO ME. I TRUSTED MOM. SO I OPENED MY FIRST SAVINGS ACCOUNT WITH FIVE DOLALRS.

WHENEVER I GOT SOME MONEY AHEAD, I'D GO AND MAKE A DEPOSIT AT THE BANK. THE FEW DOLLARS THAT I WAS PUTTING IN THE BANK SOMEHOW MADE ME FEEL LIKE I WAS DOING SOMETHING.

SOME OF THE PAPERBOYS HAD CUSTOMERS THAT WERE POOR PAYERS, THEY'D STALL AND MAYBE NEVER PAY. THOSE WOULD BE DROPPED AFTER TWO OR THREE WEEKS. I WAS VERY LUCKY, NOBODY ON MY ROUTE WAS EVER DROPPED. THERE WASN'T ANY NEW HOMES BEING BUILT IN MY AREA AND SO FOR THE NEXT THREE YEARS I MADE A DOLLAR A WEEK.

THE DEPRESSION TOUCHED JUST ABOUT EVERYONE. IT WAS A HARD TIME AND MUCH HARDER ON SOME.

I GUESS I MATURED MORE IN 1933 AND THE FOLLOWING YEARS THEN IN ANY OTHER TIME IN MY LIFE.

I LEARNED THAT IT TOOK HARD WORK TO MAKE MONEY AND I WOULDN'T SPEND IT UNLESS IT WAS NECESSARY.

MY FOLKS AND MY JOB TAUGHT ME COURTSEY AND RESPECT FOR OTHERS. MANY FRIENDSHIPS HAVE STOOD THE TEST OF TIME. IMPRESSIONS, VALUES AND OTHER THINGS THAT I LEARNED BY THE TIME I WAS TEN YEARS OLD HAVE PRETTY MUCH STUCK WITH ME THROUGH THE YEARS. I GUESS THIS WOULD BE TRUE FOR ALMOST EVERYONE IF THEY'D THINK HARD ENOUGH ABOUT IT......

AND HIS NAME WAS BUSTER

IT WAS A SATURDAY IN LATE APRIL, 1934. THE DAY WAS VERY WINDY AND KINDA CHILLY. I WAS OUT IN A LARGE FIELD WITH TWO OF MY PALS, FLYING KITES. WE HAD TO TIE LOTS OF TAILS TO OUR KITES SO THEY WOULDN'T DO LOOP THE LOOPS AND CRASH, WE WERE WORKING HARD AND HAVING FUN. WHEN THE SUN GOT HIGH, NONE OF US HAD A WATCH, WE DECIDED TO TAKE A BREAK AND GO HOME AND HAVE SOME LUNCH.

BILLY WAS NINE, JOE AND I WERE BOTH TEN. WE'D GET TOGETHER LATER AND FIGURE SOMETHING ELSE TO DO. WE STARTED REELING IN OUR KITES.

WE HAD JUST GOTTEN OUR KITES ON THE GROUND WHEN JOE HOLLERED, HEY YOU GUYS, COME OVER HERE, I WANT TO SHOW YOU SOMETHING. JOE WAS A LITTLE WAYS OFF FROM BILLY AND ME, SO WE PICKED UP OUR KITES AND WALKED OVER TO WHERE JOE WAS STANDING. WE BOTH LOOKED AT JOE AND BILLY ASKED, WHAT?

JOE ANSWERED BY POINTING AT A CLUMP OF WEEDS. WE ALL MOVED IN CLOSER TO THE WEEDS TO HAVE A LOOK. I THOUGHT THAT MAYBE JOE WAS TRYING TO PULL A GAG ON US, HE WAS ALWAYS JOKING AROUND.

THERE IN THE WEEDS LAY A SMALL BUNDLE OF FUR ROLLED UP INTO A LITTLE BALL. JOE ASKED, WHAT DO YOU THINK IT IS?

WELL, I ANSWERED, IT'S EITHER A SMALL ANIMAL OF SOME KIND OR A GIRLS HANDMUFF THAT WAS LOST LAST WITNER.

BILLY FOUND A LONG STICK AND GENTLY POKED AT THE BALL OF FUR. IT HEAVED A SIGH BUT DIDN'T WAKE UP OR TRY TO GET AWAY. AT LEAST NOW WE KNEW THAT IT WAS ALIVE. BILLY WENT TO WORK WITH HIS STICK TRYING TO TURN THE BODY OVER. WHEN HE FINALLY MANAGED TO ROLL IT OVER ONTO ITS SIDE, IT FLATTENED OUT.

MY EYES OPENED WIDE AND I SAID, WELL I'LL BE, IT'S A LITTLE DOG, AND FROM THE LOOKS OF IT, IT HASN'T HAD A GOOD MEAL LATELY. IT WAS SO THIN THAT WE COULD COUNT ALL OF ITS RIBS.

JOE WAS STARING DOWN AT IT AND SAID, HE'S A LITTLE BOY DOG.

THE DOG DIDN'T OPEN HIS EYES AND WAS SUCH A SAD LOOKING SIGHT THAT NONE OF US SAID ANYTHING MORE FOR A COUPLE OF MINUTES.

FINALLY I SAID IN KIND OF A LOW VOICE, I THINK THAT HE'S HAD SO MANY BAD THINGS HAPPEN TO HIM, HE WAS LOST WITH NO FOOD AND PROBABLY VERY LITTLE WATER FOR SO LONG THAT HE JUST GAVE UP AND CRAWLED INTO THESE WEEDS TO DIE.

BOTH BOYS GAVE ME SHOCKED LOOKS.

WELL I SHRUGGED, THAT'S THE WAY IT LOOKS TO ME.

BILLY ASKED, WHAT DO YOU THNK WE SHOULD DO?

I TOOK OFF MY JACKET AND SPREAD IT OUT NEXT TO THE LITTLE BODY AND SAID, I'M GOING TO TAKE HIM HOME AND SEE WHAT MY MOTHER THINKS. MOM WAS BORN AND RAISED ON A FARM IN IOWA. DAD CAME FROM THE SAME AREA.

THEY BOTH KNEW ABOUT GROWING THINGS AND ALL ABOUT ANIMALS.

WE LAID THE LITTLE DOG ON MY JACKET AND I CARRIED IT IN BOTH HANDS. BILLY BROUGHT ALONG MY KITE AND WE WALKED THE FOUR BLOCKS TO MY BACKYARD. I PUT MY JACKET WITH THE LITTLE BODY IN IT ON THE

GROUND NEXT TO THE BACK PORCH AND THEN WENT INTO THE HOUSE TO GET MY MOTHER.

MOM WAS IN THE KITCHEN MAKING SOUP AND SANDWICHES FOR LUNCH. I TOLD HER ABOUT THE LITTLE DOG THAT WE FOUND IN THE WEEDS AND THAT I HAD BROUGHT IT HOME.

MOM LOOKED AT ME AND SAID, WELL THEN; I'D BETTER HAVE A LOOK AT IT. WHEN SHE LOOKED DOWN AT THE LITTLE DOG SHE SAID, OH MY, I'LL BE RIGHT BACK AND HURRIED INTO THE HOUSE.

WHILE SHE WAS GONE, NONE OF US BOYS SAID ANYTHING. WE JUST KINDA STARED DOWN AT THE LITTLE DOG IN SILENCE.

MOM WAS BACK IN A FEW MINUTES CARRYING A GLASS OF WATER AND AN EYEDROPPER. SHE KNELT DOWN NEXT TO THE LITTLE FELLA AND PUT HER HAND ON HIS CHEST AND THEN SAID, THERE'S A TINY HEARTBEAT AND IT'S STEADY.

THIS MADE THE THREE OF US GUYS FEEL MUCH BETTER. I THINK THAT WE HAD ALL BEEN HOLDING OUR BREATHS UP UNTIL THEN. WE MOVED IN A LITTLE CLOSER.

MOM WENT ON, I THINK THAT HE HAS A VERY STRONG HEART TO HAVE GONE THROUGH THE HARDSHIPS THAT MUST HAVE HAPPENED TO HIM AND STILL BE ALIVE.

SHE FILLED THE EYE DROPPER WITH WATER FROM THE GLASS, OPENED HIS MOUTH A LITTLE WITH TWO FINGERS AND DRIBBLED SOME OF THE WATER ON HIS TONGUE AND THE REST AROUND IN HIS MOUTH. NEXT SHE SPRAYED SOME ON HIS NOSE AND AROUND BOTH OF HIS EYES. SHE REPEATEDLY PUT MORE WATER ON HIS TONGUE AND ASKED ME TO WATCH AND SEE IF HIS THROAT MOVED ANY. IT DIDN'T. SHE SAID THAT HIS TONGUE AND MOUTH WERE PROBABLY ABSORBING MOST OF THE WATER. SHE THEN ASKED ME TO GO DOWN INTO THE BASEMENT AND GET A SMALL CARDBOARD BOX FROM THE PILE NEXT TO THE COALBIN.

WHEN I GOT BACK WITH THE BOX SHE WAS TEARING AN OLD SHEET INTO STRIPS. SHE PUT THE RAGS INTO THE BOX AND FLUFFED THEM UP AND SAID, THAT SHOULD BE COMFORTABLE FOR HIM AND ADDED THAT THE BOYS HAD GONE HOME AND WOULD CALL ME LATER.

THE LITTLE DOG HADN'T OPENED HIS EYES SINCE WE FOUND HIM, HE HADN'T MOVED AT ALL. HIS SHALLOW BREATHING AND THE SMALL MOVEMENT OF HIS CHEST WERE THE ONLY SIGNS OF LIFE IN HIM.

MOM SAID, I THINK IT WILL BE EASIER DOING FOR HIM IF WE PUT HIM IN THE BOX AND TAKE HIM UP ON THE PORCH, WHICH WE DID. I CARRIED THE BOX UP TO THE BACK PORCH, IT DIDN'T SEEM TO WEIGH ANYTHING, AND SET IT ON A TABLE THAT MOM KEPT SOME OF HER PLANTS ON IN THE SUMMERTIME.

THE PORCH WAS INCLOSED AND WAS MOSTLY WINDOWS ABOUT THAT TIME DAD ARRIVED HOME FROM DOING SOME ERRANDS, HE LIKE TO HANG AROUND THE CORNER GAS STATION AND TALK TO THE MEN THERE. I EXPLAINED TO HIM HOW WE HAD FOUND THE DOG AND BROUGHT HIM HOME, HE LOOKED DOWN AT ATHE PITYFUL LITTLE DOG FOR ABOUT A MINUTE. HE DIDN'T SHAKE HIS HEAD OR SAY ANYTHING, HE JUST TURNED AROUND AND WALKED INTO THE HOUSE. I KNEW THAT HE WAS THINKING THAT IT WAS A LOST CAUSE.

WELL, I WASN'T GOING TO GIVE UP AND I WAS SURE THAT MOM WOULDN'T EITHER, WE ATE OUR LUNCH. DAD WENT OUT TO THE GARAGE TO TINKER WITH THE CAR. MOM SAID TO ME, GO DOWN TO MY FRUIT CELLAR AND GET A JAR OF CHICKEN BROTH, WE'LL TRY TO GIVE HIM A LITTLE NURISHMENT.

THERE WAS A LITTLE ROOM DOWN IN THE BASEMENT THAT MOM CALLED HER FRUIT CELLAR. IT WAS LINED WITH SHELVES WHERE MOM STORED THE JARS OF FRUITS, JELLY, VEGETABLES AND OTHER THINGS THAT SHE CANNED WHEN THEY WERE IN SEASON. I GUESS SHE GOT IN THE HABIT OF DOING THIS FROM GROWING UP ON THE FARM. MOM OPENED UP THE JAR OF BROTH AND HEATED IT ON THE KITCHEN STOVE FOR A COUPLE OF MINUTES AND THEN STUCK A FINGER IN IT TO TEST THE WARMTH OF IT. SHE EXPLAINED, WE DON'T WANT TO BURN HIS TONGUE OR MOUTH, AS TENDER AND SORE AS THEY MUST BE.

SHE DID THE SAME WITH THE BROTH AS SHE HAD WITH THE WATER, SHE DRIBBLED HALF A DROPPER ON HIS TONGUE, THEN WAITED A MINUTE AND EMPTIED THE REST INTO HIS MOUTH. THERE WAS NO MOVEMENT OF HIS THROAT.

IT WAS AFTER SUPPER WHEN THE BOYS CALLED. FIRST BILLY, I TOLD HIM THAT THERE WAS NO CHANGE. WHEN JOE CALLED, HE ASKED, HOW IS LITTLE BUSTER DOING? AFTER WE HUNG UP I THOUGHT TO MYSELF, WE DON'T KNOW HIS REAL NAME AND BUSTER SEEMED TO FIT HIM, SO I STARTED CALLING HIM LITTLE BUSTER. AFTER A TIME, EVERYONE WAS CALLING HIM BUSTER. HE NOW HAD A NAME, WHICH I THOUGHT GAVE HIM IDENTITY.

WE WERE WATERING BUSTER ON THE HOUR AND BOTHERING HIM ON THE HALF HOUR. MOM WANTED HIM TO DO HIS BUSNESS. SHE SAID THAT IT WOULD TELL US THAT HIS LITTLE BODY WAS FUNCTIONING. HIS BOX STAYED CLEAN. I FIGURED THAT MAYBE HIS INSIDES WERE ABSORBING THE FLUIDS WE WERE GIVING HIM. HE JUST NEEDED TIME. AT BEDTIME I ASKED MOM IF I COULD PUT THE BOX IN MY BEDROOM, IN CASE I WOKE UP DURING THE NIGHT I COULD GIVE HIM SOME WATER.

SHE SAID NO, WE'LL LEAVE HIM ON THE PORCH TONIGHT. WE'LL CLOSE THE PORCH DOOR AND OPEN TWO WINDOWS A LITTLE. HE'S VERY DIRTY, WE'LL CLEAN HIM UP TOMORROW. SHE WAS TALKING POSITIVE, LIKE SHE WAS SURE THAT HE'D STILL BE HERE TOMORROW.

I FIGURED MAYBE SHE THOUGHT HE MIGHT DIE DURING THE NIGHT AND IT WOULD BE HARD FOR ME TO DEAL WITH.

SHE GAVE ME A SERIOUS LOOK AND SAID, I DON'T KNOW IF WE CAN SAVE THIS POOR LITTLE FELLA, BUT I'LL DO EVERYTHING I CAN. I'LL NEED A LOT OF HELP FROM YOU. I NODDED YES AND SAID, I'LL DO ANYTHING YOU ASK ME TO DO.

HER REPLY WAS, GOOD. IF YOU WAKE UP DURING THE NIGHT DON'T GIVE HIM ANYTHING. WE'LL GIVE HIS BODY A CHANCE TO SEE WHAT IT CAN DO.

IN THE MORNING IT LOOKED LIKE HE HADN'T MOVED AT ALL AND HIS BED WAS CLEAN. IT WAS SUNDAY AND AFTER CHURCH SOME OF US BOYS USUALLY WENT OVER TO THE CORNER DRUGSTORE AND BOUGHT SODAS OR ICE CREAM AND FOOLED AROUND FOR A WHILE. THAT SUNDAY MORNING I WENT RIGHT STRAIGHT HOME FROM CHURCH. I FOUND MOM OUT ON THE PORCH PICKING BURRS OUT OF BUSTERS COAT. AS SOON AS I HAD CHANGED MY CLOTHES I WENT OUT AND HELPED HER. BUSTERS COAT WAS GETTING PRETTY CHOPPED UP BECAUSE MOM HAD TO CUT SO MUCH OF IT OUT TO GET TO THE BURRS. HE HAD BROWN CURLY THICK HAIR AND SOME OF IT WAS SO TANGLED WITH BURRS THAT IT HAD TO BE CUT AWAY. MOM SNIPPED AND PICKED.

AFTER WE HAD CLEARD THE BURRS AND STICKERS OUT OF BUSTERS COAT WE WENT INTO THE KITCHEN WHERE MOM PREPARED A BASIN OF WARM SOAPY WATER AND ANOTHER ONE OF CLEAR WATER. WE CARRIED THEM OUT TO THE PORCH AND MOM PROCEEDED, VERY GENTLY TO PAT AND WASH BUSTERS BODY. NEXT SHE TOWELED HIM DRY AND APPLIED VASOLINE TO THE PADS OF HIS FEET, ON HIS NOSE AND A LITTLE IN HIS EARS. I THOUGHT THAT HE LOOKED KINDA PRETTY. HIS ONLY MOVEMENT ALL THIS TIME WAS HIS SHALLOW BREATHING.

WHEN I THOUGHT ABOUT THE FOLLOWING DAY, WHICH WAS MONDAY, IT KINDA WORRIED ME. BOTH MOM AND DAD WORKED, AND WERE GONE ALL DAY. AND I WAS AT SCHOOL UNTIL THREE O'CLOCK. I DIDN'T WANT TO LEAVE BUSTER ALONE THAT LONG. I GAVE IT A LOT OF THOUGHT AND FIGURED OUT A PLAN. I TOLD MOM ABOUT MY PLAN AND ASKED HER IF I COULD TRY IT. THE PALN WAS, I'D TAKE ONLY A SANDWICH TO SCHOOL WITH ME AND EAT IT AT FIRST RECESS. I'D RUN HOME AT LUNCH TIME, IT WAS ONLY FIVE BLOCKS, GIVE BUSTER SOME FLUIDS AND MAKE SURE THAT HE WAS ALRIGHT, THEN RUN BACK TO SCHOOL.

MOM GAVE ME A LONG LOOK AND SAID, WELL, IF YOU THINK THAT YOU CAN MAKE IT ON TIME OK, BUT IF YOU'RE LATE FOR SCHOOL, THAT'LL BE THE LAST TIME I DID EXACTLY AS I TOLD MOM THAT I WOULD. I ATE MY SANDWICH AT RECESS BREAK, AND AT NOON I RAN

HOME. I GAVE LITTLE BUSTER SOME WATER AND WHILE WAITING THE FEW MINUTES BETWEEN FEEDINGS, I HAD SOME COOKIES AND MILK. WHEN I GAVE BUSTER THE BROTH I THOUGHT I SAW HIS THROAT MOVE. I GOT BACK TO THE SCHOOL PLAYGROUND AS THE FIRST BELL WAS RINGING, WHICH MEANT THAT I HAD FIVE MINUTES TO SPARE.

THAT EVENING WHEN MOM GOT HOME FROM WORK I TOLD HER THAT EVERYTING HAD WORKED OUT FINE AND THAT I THOUGHT THAT I HAD SEEN BUSTERS THROAT MOVE WHEN I GAVE HIM THE BROTH.

SHE SMILED AND SAID, GOOD, GOOD.

THAT AFTERNOON AND EVEING WHEN WE FED HIM, HIS THROAT DID MOVE AND ALSO HIS TONGUE A LITTLE. HIS EYES NEVER OPENED AND HIS BODY HAD NEVER MOVED, EVEN A LITTLE BIT.

THE FOLLOWING MORNING MOM TURNED ON MY BEDROOM LIGHT AND CALLED ME TO BREAKFAST.

FIRST THING I DID WAS TO LOOK IN ON BUSTER, AS I ALWAYS DID. HIS EYES WERE OPEN IN A FIXED STARE. I PUT MY HAND ON HIS TINY CHEST TO DETERMINE IF HE WAS BREATHING. HE WAS, AND AN ODOR COMING FROM HIS BOX ALMOST KNOCKED ME OVER. IT WAS THE SWEETEST BAD ODOR I HAD EVER SMELT. HE HAD DONE

HIS BUSINESS. I COULDN'T THINK OF ANYTHNG IN THE WORLD THAT COULD HAVE MADE ME HAPPIER.

I RUSHED OUT TO THE KITCHEN TO TELL MOM ABOUT HIS EYES AND THE ODOR. MOM SAID THAT'S WONDERFUL, HIS BODY IS STARTING TO FUNCTION, AND WE GAVE EACH OTHER A BIG HUG.

I WENT DOWNSTAIRS AND GOT A NEW BOX AND SOME CLEAN RAGS WHILE MOM WAS CLEANING HIM UP.

HIS EYES WERE STILL OPEN BUT WERE GLAZED OVER. I FIGURED THAT HE WASN'T SEEING MUCH, IF ANYTHING. HE HAD BEEN SO CLOSE TO THE EDGE AND NOW HE WAS COMING BACK. MOM AND I WERE GOING TO MAKE IT WORK. AT LEAST THAT WAS MY HOPE.

AFTER SCHOOL I TOOK THE BOX OUT TO THE BACK YARD. IT WAS A NICE WARM SUNNY DAY. MOM HAD GIVEN ME AN OLD CLEAN BATH TOWEL. I SPREAD THE TOWEL ON THE GRASS AND LIFTED BUSTER OUT OF THE BOX AND LAID HIM ON IT. THEN I WENT DOWN IN THE BASEMENT AND GOT THE PICNIC BLANKET NEXT TO BUSTERS TOWEL AND STRETCHED OUT ON IT. I MUST HAVE DOZED OFF BECAUSE THE NEXT THING I KNEW, MOM WAS STANDING OVER ME SAYING, MY, YOU BOYS SURE LOOK COMFORTABLE.

THE NEXT DAY WAS THURSDAY, THINGS WENT ALONG ABOUT THE SAME AS USUAL. WHEN I PUT BUSTER ON THE TOWEL IN THE BACK YARD, HE LOOKED RIGHT AT

ME I WAS SURE THAT HIS EYES WERE FOCUSING AND HE COULD SEE ME. HE KEPT STARING AT ME AS THOUGH HE WAS TRYING TO FIGURE OUT WHO I WAS, I LAY DOWN ON THE BLANKET AND REACHED OVER WITH BOTH HANDS AND LIFTED HIM AND SET HIM ON MY CHEST.

HE STRETCHED HIS NECK UP SO AS TO SEE MY FACE. I MOVED HIS BODY AROUND SO THAT HE COULD. HE LOOKED AT ME FOR A MINUTE OR TWO, THEN HE PUT HIS CHEEK ON MY CHEST AND CLOED HIS EYES. I GUESS HE HAD DETERMINED THAT HE COULD TRUST ME. I PULLED MY BASEBALL CAP DOWN OVER MY EYES AND JOINED HIM IN SLUMBER.

LATER, WHEN I TOLD MOM WHAT HAD HAPPENED, SHE SAID, I THINK MAYBE IT'S TIME TO TRY SOME SOLID FOOD ON HIM.

I FOLLOWED HER INTO THE KITCHEN AND SAT DOWN AT THE TABLE. I HAD SOME HOMEWORK TO DO, BUT I WATCHED HER FROM THE CORNER OF MY EYE.

SHE POURED SOME OF THE CHICKEN BROTH INTO A PAN AND PUT IT ON THE STOVE, THEN SHE GOT A LARGE HANDFUL OF HAMBURGER MEAT OUT OF THE FRIDGE AND CHOPPED IT UP REAL FINE AND ADDED IT TO THE BROTH AND TURNED THE HEAT UP ON HIGH UNDER THE PAN. WHEN THE BROTH BEGAN TO BOIL SHE TURNED THE HEAT DOWN TO SIMMER. AS THE MEAT WAS COOKING SHE STARTED PREPARING SUPPER.

FIRST SHE PEELED SOME POTATOES AND HALVED THEM AND PUT THEM IN A PAN OF WATER TO COOK. WE WERE GOING TO HAVE FIRED HAMBURGER PADDIES IN WHITE GRAVY, SWEET PEAS AND BOILED POTATOES, TOPPED OFF WITH HOME MADE APPLE PIE WITH A SCOOP OF ICE-CREAM ON IT. A GREAT MEAL.

DAD HAD GOTTEN HOME FROM WORK AND WAS SITTING ON THE PORCH READING THE EVENING NEWSPAPER. I HAD FINISHED MY HOMEWORK SO I SET THE TABLE. AFTER SUPPER, MOM WASHED THE DISHES AND I DRIED THEM AND PUT THEM AWAY. SHE HAD TURNED OFF THE BURNER UNDER THE BROTH SOME TIME BEFORE AND IT HAD COOLED DOWN QUITE A BIT.

MOM HAD ME TAKE BUSTERS BOX AND TOWEL OUT TO THE BACKYARD. SHE CAME OUT IN A WHILE WITH A BOWL OF THE BROTH AND MEAT AND TOLD ME TO HOLD BUSTER UPRIGHT ON THE TOWEL. HE DIDN'T HAVE TO BE STANDING, JUST UPRIGHT.

I GOT BEHIND HIM AND PUT BOTH OF MY HANDS UNDER HIS CHEST AND STOMACH, HE WAS PRETTY FLOPSY. I LIFTED HIM SO THAT HE WAS IN THE STANDING POSITION WITH IS FRONT LEGS AND HIS HIND QUARTERS WERE SITTING.

MOM KNELT DOWN IN FRONT OF HIM AND HELD UP HIS HEAD WITH ONE HAND AND TOOK A TINY PINCH OF THE HAMBURGER BROTH BETWEEN THE FINGERS OF HER OTHER HAND AND PUT IT ON BUSTERS TONGUE.

HIS MOUTH GAVE A SMALL CHEWING MOTION AND HIS THROAT MOVED. SHE GAVE HIM MORE PINCHES AND BY THIS TIME, HIS MOUTH WAS DOING SOME REAL CHEWING.

BUSTER NEVER TOOK HIS EYES OFF OF MOMS FACE. IT WAS LIKE HE WAS SAYING, I CAN TASTE IT, I LIKE IT, AND I WANT MORE. I THINK MOM MADE A LIFE LONG FRIEND THAT DAY. A FEW MINUTES AFTER FEEDING HIM, SHE TOLD ME TO GIVE HIM SOME WATER AND ADDED, WE'LL GIVE THE FOOD TIME TO SETTLE AND IF IT SETS WELL, WE'LL GIVE HIM MORE LATER. HE DIDN'T GET SICK AND SEEMED RELAXED AND LOOKED BETTER THAN HE EVER HAD. HE KNEW HE WAS HUNGRY AND WANTED MORE OF THE GREATEST FOOD HE PROBABLY EVER TASTED. MOM WARNED ME NOT TO OVER DO IT, JUST FIVE OR SIX PINCHES AT A TIME, FOLLOWED BY WATER. PLENTY OF WATER.

I FED HIM IN THE MORNING AND AT LUNCHTIME. HE SEEMED TO KNOW WHEN I'D BE HOME FOR LUNCH. HE ALWAYS LOOKED AT ME AFTER I FINISHED FEEDING HIM. HIS EYES KEPT SAYING, I CAN USE A LOT MORE. THINGS WERE GOING ALONG TOO GOOD FOR ME TO GIVE IN TO HIM AND GIVE HIM MORE. MOM KNEW WHAT WAS BEST.

AFTER SCHOOL THAT DAY, I TOOK BUSTER OUT TO HE BACKYARD AND FED HIM ON HIS TOWEL. HE DIDN'T NEED ANYONE TO HOLD HIS HEAD UP BY THEN, HE WAS READY TO BE FED. HE SAT ON HIS HIND QUARTERS AND STOOD UP ON HIS FRONT LEGS. THAT WAY OF EATING

WAS A HABIT THAT STAYED WITH HIM FOR THE REST OF HIS LIFE.

AFTER PUTTNG HIS FEED DOWN, I LAY DOWN ON THE BLANKET, ABOUT THREE FEET FROM HIS TOWEL AND LOOKED UP AT THE PASSING CLOUDS IN A VERY BLUE SKY.

IN A FEW MINUTES I FELT SOMETHING ON MY ARM, I TURNED MY HEAD TO SEE WHAT IT WAS, THERE SAT BUSTER, WITH BOTH OF HIS FRONT FEET LAYING LIGHTLY ON MY ARM. I FELT A KIND OF CHILL AND THOUGHT ABOUT THE DAY THAT WE FOUND HIM. IT MADE MY HEAD SPIN TO THINK ABOUT IT, WHAT IF JOE HADN'T BEEN FLYING HIS KITE AWAY FROM BILLY AND ME. WE MIGHT NEVER HAVE FOUND BUSTER, MAYBE NOBODY ELSE WOULD HAVE FOUND HIM EITHER.

THERE NEVER WOULD HAVE BEEN THIS LITTLE DOG WITH THE CHOPPED UP HAIRCUT IN MY LIFE. HE AND I BOTH WOULD HAVE MISSED SO VERY MUCH. THE PLEASURE OF KNOWING HIM AND BEING WITH HIM, BROUGHT A WHOLE NEW PROSPECTIVE TO MY LIFE.

I LEARNED SO MUCH ABOUT LIFE IN THAT ONE WEEK WHEN I WAS TEN YEARS OLD THAT I CAN'T RECOUNT IT ALL. THERE WAS RESPONSIBILITY, RESPECT FOR OTHERS INCLUDING ALL ANIMALS, PATIENCE AND MANY OTHER THINGS THAT HAVE SERVED ME WELL EVER AFTER. THANK YOU JOE AND BILLY, THANK YOU MOM AND THANK YOU LITTLE BUSTER......

A SPECIAL TIME AND PLACE

IT WAS NINE IN THE EVENING AND HAD BEEN SNOWING FOR AN HOUR THERE WAS LITTLE WIND AND THE BIG SNOWFLAKES GENTLY FLOATED DOWN AND QUICKLY COVERED THE GROUND. I HAD GONE OUT TO GATHER FIREWOOD AND WAS PERHAPS FORTY YARDS FROM CAMP. IT WAS 1935 AND I WAS TWELVE YEARS OLD.

ALTHOUGH THE CAMPFIRE WAS FAIRLY LARGE, THROUGH THE TREES AND FALLING SNOW IT NOW LOOKED SMALL AND TWINKLY AND DISTANT.

THE FULL MOON WASN'T HIGH, IT APPEARED TO BE VERY CLOSE AND I THOUGHT IT'S GREAT SIZE THREATENED TO COMPETELY FILL THE ENTIRE SKY. THE LIGHT THROWN OUT BY THE MOON REFLECTED OFF THE SNOW ON THE GROUND AND GAVE ME THE FEELING OF BEING IN A DAY-NIGHT UNKNOWN PLACE. ALONE. THE NIGHT WAS CALM AND SERENE AND WHEN I TURNED MY FACE SKYWARD, THE HUGE SNOWFLAKES LANDED ON MY FACE AND CLUNG TO MY EYELASHES.

Ronald M. Gifford

I HAD A STRANGE FEELING OF PEACEFULNESS AND WARMTH. THE REALIZATION CAME TO ME THAT FOR A FEW SHORT MOMENTS, I HAD BEEN PUT INTO A VERY WONDERFUL AND SPECIAL TIME AND PLACE......

BEING HONEST IS THE EASIEST WAY

FROM THE TIME I WAS OLD ENOUGH TO UNDERSTAND AND REMEMBER THINGS, MY PARENTS AND MY GRANDMOTHER ALL KEPT TELLING ME THAT HONESTY WAS THE BEST WAY TO BE. NOT TELLING LIES WAS A LOT EASIER THAN LYING. WHEN YOU LIED YOU MIGHT HURT SOMEBODY ELSE AND THEN YOU'D FEEL BAD ABOUT IT.

MOM TOLD ME THAT IF I WAS ALWAYS HONEST AND TRUTHFUL ABOUT EVERYTHING WITH EVERYONE, IT WOULD MEAN THAT I WAS BEING HONEST WITH MYSELF AND I'D ALWAYS HAVE A CLEAR CONSCIENCE AND THAT WAS THE IMPORTANT THING. IF I MADE A MISTAKE OR DID SOMETHING WRONG AND ADMITTED TO IT, I'D HAVE TO TAKE WHATEVER PUNISHMENT THAT WAS CALLED FOR, THEN I COULD GO ON WITH MY LIFE. IT SOUNDED TO ME LIKE IT WAS THE RIGHT THING TO DO.

WHEN I WAS EIGHT YEARS OLD I HAD MY FIRST REAL TEST WITH HONESTY. TOM, EARL AND I WERE FRIENDS THAT LIVED ON THE SAME STREET. WE WALKED TO AND FROM SCHOOL MOST OF THE TIME TOGETHER. WE ALL LOVED BASEBALL AND WE TALKED A LOT ABOUT

THE CHICAGO TEAMS, THE CUBS AND WHITESOX. WE PLAYED A LOT OF CATCH AND PRACTICED HITTING AND FIELDING GROUND BALLS AND FLY BALLS. SOMETIMES OTHER KIDS WOULD JOIN US.

ONE EARLY SPRING DAY WE WERE WALKING HOME ON 61ST STREET. 61ST STREET WAS THE LAST STREET IN OUR NEIGHBORHOOD TO BE PAVED. IT WAS STILL A GRAVEL ROAD. SOME OF THE GRAVEL WAS PRETTY GOOD SIZE ROCKS WE WERE THROWING THESE BIGGER ROCKS AT TELEPHONE POLES, LAMP POSTS AND TREES. IT WAS A GAME WE PLAYED, TRYING TO BE THE MOST ACCURATE WITH OUR THROWS. I WAS THE FIRST TO THROW AT A TREE THAT WAS STANDING ABOUT SIX FEET FROM A HOUSE. I HIT THE TREE ALRIGHT, BUT HE ROCK CAROMED OFF THE TREE AND BROKE A BASEMENT WINDOW OF THE HOUSE. MY TWO FRIENDS TOOK OFF RUNNING. I JUST STOOD THERE, GLUED TO THE SPOT.

I KNEW RIGHT AWAY THAT I HAD DONE SOMETHING WRONG AND WOULD HAVE TO ANSWER FOR IT. I THOUGHT THAT SOMEONE WOULD COME OUT OF THE HOUSE AND GRAB ME OR HOLLER, BUT NOBODY CAME OUT. AFTER WAITING THERE A FEW MINUTES I PROCEEDED TO WALK SLOWLY HOME. I COULDN'T THINK WHAT I WAS SUPPOSE TO DO. WHEN I GOT HOME, MOM WAS IN THE KITCHEN PREPARING ONE OF MY FAVORITE DINNERS, HAMBURGER AND SPAGHETTI IN TOMATO SAUCE AND HOME MADE BISCUITS.

MOM, DAD, SIS AND I SAT AT THE KITHCEN TABLE AND EVERYBODY STARTED EATING. I PUT A FORK FULL OF MY SPAGHETTI INTO MY MOUTH, CHEWED IT BUT COULDN'T SWALLOW IT. I CHEWED IT SOME MORE AND WHEN I TRIED TO SWALLOW, THE SPAGHETTI STUCK IN MY THROAT IN A BIG LUMP. I CLEARED MY THROAT AND TRIED AGAIN, IT DIDN'T WORK. I SAT THERE LOOKING DOWN AT MY PLATE.

MOM LOOKED AT ME AND ASKED, IS THERE SOMETHING WRONG BUD? DON'T YOU FEEL WELL?

I DIDN'T SPEAK. I SHOOK MY HEAD A LITTLE WHILE STILL LOOKING DOWN AT MY PLATE. I FELT OVERHEATED. I'M SURE MY FACE WAS RED. MOM WAS LOOKING INTENTLY AT ME WHEN SHE SAID, COME ON BUD, LET'S GO OUT ON THE PORCH, I THINK YOU CAN USE SOME FRESH AIR. OUT ON THE PROCH, MOM LOOKED CLOSELY INTO MY FACE AND SAID, SOMETHING'S BOTHERING YOU BUD. NOW, WHAT'S WRONG?

AFTER THINKING FOR A MINUTE, I BLURTED OUT THE STORY OF THE BROKEN WINDOW. ALMOST AT ONCE, AFTER GETTING IT OFF MY CHEST, I FELT A GREAT RELIEF AND I ADDED, I DON'T KNOW WHAT TO DO. MOM SAID, THIS IS YOUR PROBLEM. IT'S ALL UP TO YOU WHAT YOU'RE GOINT TO DO ABOUT IT. NOBODY SAW YOU, SO YOU CAN JUST FORGET ABOUT IT. I THINK THAT THE RIGHT THING WOULD BE FOR YOU TO TAKE SOME OF YOUR MONEY OVER THERE. EXPLAIN WHAT HAPPENED,

APOLOGIZE AND OFFER TO PAY TO HAVE THE WINDOW REPLACED. IT'S UP TO YOU.

IT WAS ALL SO CLEAR WHEN MOM SAID IT.

I WENT AND GOT THREE DOLLARS OUT OF MY SOX DRAWER AND AS I WAS LEAVING MOM SAID, I'LL KEEP SUPPER WARM FOR YOU. WHEN I RANG THE BELL AT THE BROKEN WINDOW HOUSE, A LADY OPENED THE DOOR AND ASKED IF SHE COULD HELP ME. I TOLD HER ABOUT THE BROKEN WINDOW AND I SAID, I'M SORRY I DID IT AND I WANT TO PAY FOR IT.

SHE LOOKED AT ME FOR A MINUTE OR TWO AND ASKED, DID YOUR MOTHER OR FATHER SEND YOU HERE?

I ANSWERED NO, I CAME BECAUSE I KNOW THAT I DID WRONG AND IT'S BOTHERED ME SO MUCH SINCE IT HAPPENED THAT I WANT TO FIX IT UP WITH YOU IF I CAN. HERE'S THREE DOLLARS, IF IT'S NOT ENOUGH, I'LL COME BACK TOMORROW WITH THE REST.

SHE ASKED, IS THIS YOUR OWN MONEY?

I ANSWERED, YES MA'AM, IT IS.

SHE GAVE ME ANOTHER LONG LOOK AND SAID, YOU'RE A GOOD BOY, AND BEING THAT YOU HAVE TOLD ME WHAT HAPPENED I WANT YOU TO KEEP YOUR MONEY. MY HUSBAND CAN FIX THE WINDOW AND I KNOW

THAT YOU WON'T DO IT AGAIN. THANK YOU FOR BEING HONEST WITH ME. YOU'D BETTER GET ON HOME NOW. IT'LL BE GETTING DARK SOON.

I WAS SPEECHLESS. THERE WAS NOTHING THAT I COULD SAY BUT A WEAK THANK YOU.

I WALKED BRISKLY HOME AND FELT AS LIGHT AS A FEATHER. IT SEEMED AS THOUGH A GREAT WEIGHT HAD BEEN LIFTED OFF OF ME AND IT WAS A NEW AWAKENING FOR ME.

NOW I KNEW FOR SURE THAT THE THINGS THAT MY FOLKS AND MY GRANDMOTHER HAD BEEN TELLING ME WERE RIGHT ON THE MARK.

BEING HONEST WAS THE BEST AND EASIEST WAY TO LIVE......

A SUMMER DAY

THE SUN WAS VERY BRIGHT AS IT STREAMED IN THROUGH MY WINDOW, IT WOKE ME UP. THE MORNING WAS ALREADY HOT AND IT LOOKED LIKE THE DAY WAS GOING TO BE A REAL SCORCHER, BUT IT REALLY DIDN'T MATTER. I KNEW IT WAS GOING TO BE A GREAT DAY AS LONG AS IT DIDN'T RAIN.

CONEY ISLAND IN NEW YORK WAS BILLED AS THE BEST AMUSEMENT PARK IN AMERICA, BUT RIVERVIEW PARK WAS KNOWN AS THE BIGGEST AND WE HAD IT RIGHT IN CHICAGO.

FIVE OF US PALS FROM THE NEIGHBORHOOD HAD BEEN LOOKING FORWARD TO THIS DAY FOR A LONG TIME. WE WERE GOING TO RIVERVIEW AND IT WAS TWO CENTS A DAY.

OUR BUNGALOW ON THE SOUTHWEST SIDE OF THE CITY HAD JUST TWO BEDROOMS. ONE WAS MY PARENTS ROOM AND THE OTHER WAS MY SISTERS.

IN COLD WEATHER I SLEPT ON THE STUDIO COUCH IN THE DINNING ROOM AND THE REST OF THE YEAR I SLEPT ON THE DAYBED ON THE SUN PORCH AT THE BACK OF THE HOUSE WHICH FACED EAST. I SHARED A DRESSER AND A CLOSET WITH MY SISTER IN HER ROOM. I REMEMBER WHEN I WAS REALLY SMALL WE LIVED IN A TWO BEDROOM APARTMENT. MY FOLKS USED TO SHOVE TWO OVER STUFFED CHAIRS TOGETHER IN THE FRONT ROOM. EVERY EVENING MOM MADE IT UP AS A BED WITH SHEETS, BLANKET AND PILLOW, AND THAT'S WHERE I SLEPT.

WE LIVED IN SEVERAL APARTMENTS AND HOUSES WHILE I WAS GROWING UP AND NONE OF THEM EVER HAD MORE THEN TWO BEDROOMS. I DON'T EVER REMEMBER BEING MAD OR REGRETTING THAT I DIDN'T HAVE A ROOM OF MY OWN.

YEARS LATER WHEN MY SISTER GOT MARRIED, I TOOK OVER HER ROOM. IT WAS 1941 AND I WAS A JUNIOR IN HIGH SCHOOL. TWO YEARS LATER THE SECOND WORLD WAR WAS BOOMING AND I JOINED THE U. S. NAVY. IN BOOT CAMP IN THE NAVY I SHARED A BIG BARRACKS ROOM WITH A HUNDRED AND NINETEEN OTHER GUYS AND WHEN I WAS ABOARD SHIP MY SLEEPING COMPARTMENT SLEPT ABOUT TWENTY MEN.

I WAS ALWAYS AN EARLY RISER, SECOND ONLY TO MY MOTHER, WHO WOULD PUT HER COFFEE POT ON THE KITCHEN STOVE THE FIRST THING IN THE MORNING.

SHE LIKES HER COFFEE STEAMING HOT AND BLACK. THE AROMA OF THAT FRESH POT OF COFFEE IN THE MORNING WAS MY WAKE-UP CALL FOR YEARS. I DIDN'T NEED AN ALARM CLOCK OR SOMEONE SHAKING ME TO WAKE UP, THE SMELL DRIFTING IN FROM THE KITCHEN OF MOMS FRESHLY BREWED COFFEE TOLD ME IT WAS TIME TO GET UP. THE YEAR WAS 1935 AND I WAS ELEVEN YEARS OLD. I HEARD IT SAID THAT WE WERE IN A BAD DEPRESSION. WELL, THOSE WERE JUST WORDS TO US KIDS. THINGS HAD BEEN ABOUT THE SAME ALL OF OUR LIVES AND WE DIDN'T KNOW ANY OTHER TIMES. WE NEVER HAD MUCH MONEY, THAT'S THE WAY IT WAS. WE HAD OUR FRIENDS THAT WE COULD COUNT ON. THE THINGS WE DID AND THE GAMES WE PLAYED DIDN'T COST MUCH AND TOOK VERY LITTLE EQUIPMENT. I GUESS OUR FOLKS WORRIED ABOUT A LOT OF THINGS DURING THE DEPRESSION, BUT THEY NEVER BOTHERED US KIDS WITH THEIR PROBLEMS OR EXPLAINED THEM TO US EITHER.

MY DAD WAS A TRAINMAN ON A RAILROAD THAT DID WORK IN CHICAGO AND THE SURROUNDING AREAS. HE NEVER GOT LAID OFF BUT HE WAS ONLY ABLE TO WORK FROM TWO TO FOUR DAYS A WEEK. HE WAS ONE OF THE YOUNGER EMPLOYEES AND THE RAILROADS WORK STRICKLY BY SENIORITY.

MOM WORKED AT A FACTORY THAT MADE RADIOS. I HEARD THAT SHE MADE SEVEN DOLLARS A WEEK FOR FORTHY HOURS OF WORK. SEVEN DOLLARS DOESN'T

SOUND LIKE MUCH NOW, BUT YOU COULD FEED A FAMILY OF FOUR FOR FIVE OR SIX DOLLARS A WEEK IN THE EARLY 1930S. WE DIDN'T EAT FANCY BUT THERE WAS ALWAYS FOOD ON THE TABLE AND A ROOF OVER OUR HEADS. MOM WAS A GREAT COOK WHILE HAVING VERY LITTLE TO WORK WITH.

MOM USUALLY GAVE SIS AND ME A DIME SO WE COULD GO TO THE MOVIES ON SATURDAYS. I SOMETIMES TOOK A LITTLE PAPER SACK TO THE MOVIES WITH ME THAT CONTAINED HOME MADE COOKIES OR SOME FUDGE. MY SISTER THOUGHT THAT I WAS KINDA CRAZY AND WOULDN'T SIT NEAR ME DURING THE SHOW. IT WAS A LONG DAY WITH TWO FEATURED MOVIES, A CARTOON, A SERIAL, THE THREE STOOGES OR A LAUREL AND HARDY COMEDY AND A NEWS REEL, I GOT HUNGRY.

SONNY WAS A BOY WHO LIVED THREE HOUSES UP THE STREET FROM ME AND WAS A YEAR OR SO YOUNGER. HE WAS THE YOUNGEST OF FOUR BROTHER AND THREE SISTERS IN HIS FAMILY. HE WAS A GOOD BASEBALL PLAYER, TOP SPINNER AND WAS GREAT AT MUMBLY PEG. ALTHOUGH HE WAS A LITTLE YOUNGER THEN THE REST OF MY GROUP, HE WAS READILY EXCEPTED INTO IT. BEING FROM A LARGE FAMILY, I DON'T THINK THAT HE HAD A LOT OF TOYS OF HIS OWN. HE HAD WHAT MOST BOYS AT THE TIME CARRIED IN THEIR POCKETS, IN SUMMER, A TOP, A FEW MARBLES IN CASE THEY CAME ACROSS A GOOD GAME, A POCKET KNIFE AND MAYBE A YOYO.

ALL OF US GUYS MADE OUR OWN KITES. TWO SLIM GREEN WILLOW BRANCHES, ONE BRANCH WAS LONGER THEN THE OTHER AND THEY WERE FASTENED TOGETHER WITH STRING TO FORM A TEE. THIS WAS THE BASIC FORM OF THE KITE. A PIECE OF STRING WAS TIED TO ONE END OF THE SHORTER BRANCH, THEN THE BRANCH WAS BENT SO THERE WAS A TWO OR THREE BOW IN IT AND THE STRING WAS TIED TO THE OTHER END OF THE BRANCH TO HOLD THE BOW. THERE WERE SMALL NOTCHES CUT IN ALL ENDS OF THE BRANCHES. A PIECE OF STRING WAS SLIPPED INTO THE NOTCHES AROUND THE FORM AND TIED TOGETHER. NEXT, WAS STRETCHED OVER THE FORM AND DOUBLED BACK ABOUT AN INCH, CUT AND GLUED TO ITSELF. THE STRING WE USED FOR OUR KITES WAS SAVED FROM YEAR TO YEAR. YOU COULD BUY A BALL OF STRING FOR A NICKEL. THE LAST THING WAS THE TAIL. WE'D RIP OLD RAGS INTO TWO INCH WIDE STRIPS AND TIE THEM TOGETHER, THAT WAS THE TAIL. IF YOUR KITE TWISTED OVER AND OVER IN THE AIR IT MEANT THAT YOU NEEDED MORE TAIL, OR IF WHEN YOU TRIED TO FLY YOUR KITE IT STAYED FLAT AND DIDN'T GO UP, YOU HAD TOO MUCH TAIL ON IT AND NEEDED TO REMOVE SOME IF IT. YOU LEARNED THESE THINGS THROUGH TRIAL AND ERROR.

SOME TIMES IN WINTER I'D INVITE SONNY OVER TO OUR HOUSE, IT WAS MORE FUN DOING THINGS WITH OTHER PALS THEN PLAYING BY YOURSELF. WE'D GO DOWN TO THE BASEMENT AND BE IN OUR OWN LITTLE WORLD FOR A FEW HOURS.

MY ELECTRIC TRAIN WAS SET UP PERMANENTLY IN A LITTLE ROOM DOWN THERE. I HAD LINCOLN LOGS AND A LOT OF MEN OF ALL KINDS, MADE OUT OF LEAD. THERE WERE SOME COWBOYS AND INDIANS, AND HORSES AND BARN ANIMALS. WE EVEN HAD NAMES FOR SOME OF THEM. WE BUILT TOWNS AND FORTS AND CABINS AND BARNS AND CORRALS. OUR IMAGINATIONS WOULD TAKE US INTO ALL KINDS OF SITUATIONS. ONE OF US WOULD HAVE AN IDEA AND WE'D BOTH GO TO WORK ON IT.

WE WERE BOTH PRETTY SHY AND NIETHER OF US SAID MUCH, WE DIDN'T HAVE TO. WE WORKED TOGETHER SMOOTHLY.

THE MORNING WOULD END WITH MY MOTHER SERVING US SOUP AND SANWICHES AND COCOA. IT WAS A GOOD PERIOD IN BOTH OUR LIVES. AFTER SCHOOL LET OUT FOR THE SUMMER, FIVE OF US BOYS FROM THE NEIGHBORHOOD HUNG AROUND TOGETHER. WE PLAYED A LOT OF CATCH AND BASEBALL, HORSESHOES, MUMBLY PEG AND OTHER GAMES. WE JOKED AND TALKED ABOUT THINGS THAT WERE IMPORTANT TO US. THE SUBJECT OF GIRLS CAME UP ONCE IN A WHILE, BUT THAT NEVER LASTED VERY LONG. NONE OF US KNEW MUCH ABOUT GIRLS. THOSE OF US THAT HAD SISTERS KNEW THEY COULD BE A PAIN IN THE NECK SOMETIMES.

WE MADE BETS WITH EACH OTHER ON THE HORSES IN THE KENTUCKY DERBY AND WHICH BASEBALL TEAMS IN THE AMERICAN AND NATIONAL LEAGUES WOULD

WIN THE PENNANTS, THE WORLD SERIES WOULD COME LATER. WE BET ON A LOT OF THINGS, NOT FOR MONEY OR ANYTHING OF VALUE, IT WAS JUST FOR THE FUN OF IT AND THE BRAGGING RIGHTS. THE PLAN FOR THAT PARTICULAR MORNING WAS FOR SONNY TO PICK ME UP AT MY HOUSE, THEN WE'D GO TO JOES PLACE AND GET HIM AND THE THREE OF US WOULD WALK UP TO 63RD AND CENTRAL AVE. WHERE WE'D JOIN THE OTHER GUYS, JUMP ON A STREETCAR AND BE ON OUR WAY TO THE RIVERVIEW AMUSEMENT PARK. THE RIVER WAS THERE ALL RIGHT, BUT WE WERE NOT GOING THERE TO LOOK AT THE RIVER. WE WERE GOING TO THE LARGEST AMUSEMENT PARK IN THE WORLD, WITH A TWO AND A HALF MILE LONG MIDWAY, SIX OR SEVEN ROLLER COASTERS, SEVERAL FUN HOUSES, A HUGE PENNY ARCADE AND MORE GAMES, RIDES AND OTHER THINGS TO SEE AND DO THEN WE COULD POSSIBLY COVER IN A WEEK, LET ALONE A SINGLE DAY.

MOM WAS MAKING MY LUNCH IN THE KITCHEN; WE WERE ALL TAKING BROWN BAG LUNCHES. WE'D START EATING THEM ON THE LONG STREETCAR RIDE TO THE PARK AND FINISH THEM OFF SOON AFTER WE ARRIVED AT THE PARK SO THAT WE WOULDN'T HAVE TO CARRY THEM AROUND. THERE WAS A KNOCK AT THE FRONT DOOR AND WHEN I OPENED IT, SONNY WAS STANDING THERE WITH A SAD LOOK ON HIS FACE.

I SAID GOOD MORNING, COME ON IN, I'LL BE READY IN A FEW MINUTES. SONNY DIDN'T MAKE A MOVE TO COME INTO THE HOUSE.

I ASKED HIM IF THERE WAS SOMETHING WRONG.

HE ANSWERED, I DON'T KNOW IF I SHOULD GO TODAY OR NOT, I'VE ONLY GOT EIGHTEEN CENTS.

I DID SOME QUICK ARITHMETIC IN MY HEAD, SIX CENTS STREETCAR FARES AND TWO CENTS TO GET INTO THE PARK, WHICH LEFT SONNY WITH ONLY TEN CENTS. I KNEW THAT THE OTHER FELLOWS WOULDN'T FEEL RIGHT HAVING FUN PLAYING GAMES AND RIDING RIDES WITH SONNY STANDING THERE WATCHING US.

I ASKED HIM WHAT HE HAD IN HIS BAG FOR LUNCH. I WAS TRYING TO THINK OF WHAT TO DO AND HOW TO DO IT.

HE ANSWERED, A PEANUTBUTTER SANDWICH AND AN ORANGE.

I SAID, COME ON OUT TO THE KITCHEN AND I'LL GET MY LUNCH AND MONEY.

MOM PUT A BALONEY SANDWICH, A PIECE OF CAKE AND AN APPLE IN MY BAG. I SAID TO SONNY, I'LL BE RIGHT BACK AND WENT INTO MY SISTERS BEDROOM AND TOOK

MORE MONEY OUT OF MY SOCK DRAWER THEN I HAD INTENDED TO TAKE TO THE PARK.

WHEN WE WERE ON THE FRONT PORCH I CLOSED THE DOOR AND SAID, HOLD OUT YOUR HAND SONNY.

HE ASKED, WHY?

I ANSWERED, NEVER MIND WHY, JUST HOLD OUT YOUR HAND.

HE SLOWLY PUT OUT HIS RIGHT HAND AND I PUT TWO DIMES IN IT. HE LOOKED DOWN AT THE MONEY AND THEN UP AT MY FACE.

I SAID, THIS IS JUST BETWEEN TWO PALS. YOU'RE A LITTLE SHORT ON MONEY AND I'M LENDING YOU SOME. SOME TIME YOU'LL HAVE SOME EXTRA MONEY AND PAY ME BACK. FOR NOW THIS IS JUST BETWEEN YOU AND ME, WE DIDN'T TELL ANYONE ELSE ABOUT IT. HE STOOD THERE WITH HIS MOUTH OPENED A LITTLE AND DIDN'T SAY ANYTHING. I SAID, PUT IT IN YOUR POCKET AND LET'S GET GOIN. JOE'LL THINK WE GOT LOST SOME PLACE.

ABOUT TWO WEEKS EARLIER, MOM SENT ME TO THE BAKERY SHOP FOR A LOAF OF RAISIN BREAD. SHE LOVED TOASTED RASIN BREAD WITH HER MORNING COFFEE. I WAS A HALF A BLOCK FROM THE BAKERY WHEN THERE WAS A SUDDEN CLOUD BURST. THE RAIN CAME DOWN IN BUCKETS. I FELT LIKE A LITTLE PUPPY THAT

HAD ACCIDENTALLY FALLEN INTO THE LAKE AND WAS OVERWHELMED AND SHOCKED, GETTING ALL WET AND BEING ALONE IN SO MUCH WATER. HE JUST COULDN'T GET OUT OF THE LAKE FAST ENOUGH AND SHAKE HIMSELF.

I RAN AS FAST AS I COULD TO THE BAKERY AND SHOOK MYSELF AND LINGERED THERE UNTIL IT QUITE RAINING.

AFTER IT STOPPED RAINING AND I WAS WALKING HOME, I WAS THINKING ABOUT GETTING INTO SOME DRY CLOTHES MORE THAN ANYTHING ELSE. I NOTICED THAT THE STREET WAS FLOODING WITH WATER RIGHT UP TO THE TOP OF THE GUTTERS AND WAS RUNNING FAST TO THE SEWER DRAINS, CARRYING SMALL OBJECTS ALONG. WHILE WATCHING THE THINGS THAT WERE GOING DOWN THE SEWER I SPIED WHAT LOOKED LIKE A DOLLAR BILL AND I REACHED DOWN AND GRABBED THE BILL JUST BEFORE IT WENT DOWN THE SEWER. WHEN I LOOKED AT IT IN MY HAND IT TURNED OUT TO BE A FIVE DOLLAR BILL, I COULDN'T BELIEVE IT. I HAD NEVER IN MY LIFE HELD A FIVE DOLLAR BILL IN MY HANDS BEFORE AND IT GAVE ME AN EERIE DREAM LIKE FEELING. THERE WAS NO WAY OF KNOWING WHO HAD LOST IT, SO I GUESSED THAT IT WAS MINE NOW.

WHEN I GOT HOME AND TOLD MOM ABOUT IT, SHE TOOK IT AND FLATTENED IT OUT ON THE DRAIN BOARD OF THE KITCHEN SINK TO DRY AND SAID, IF I WERE YOU, I WOULDN'T TELL ANYBODY ABOUT THIS. THEY MIGHT

WANT TO BORROW SOME OF IT. I FIGURED THAT SHE WAS PROBABLY REFERING TO SIS.

MOM GOT HER PURSE AND COUNTED OUT FOUR ONE DOLLAR BILLS AND A DOLLARS WORTH OF CHANGE AND HANDED IT TO ME AND SAID, YOU'LL BE ABLE TO HANDLE IT BETTER THIS WAY.

I TUCKED THE MONEY IN MY SOCK DRAWER ALONG WITH SOME THAT WAS THERE. A LOT OF THINGS WERE GOING AROUND IN MY HEAD. A BASEBALL GLOVE, A GOOD USED BIKE OR MAYBE A PAIR OF SHOE ICESKATES. THEY'RE WOULD BE A LOT OF DAY DREAMING BEFORE I'D FINALLY MAKE UP MY MIND AS TO WHAT WAS THE MOST IMPORTANT THING TO DO WITH THE MONEY.

IT WAS A LONG HOT TRIP TO RIVERVIEW PARK. THE STREETCARS DIDN'T HAVE AIR CONDITIONING, JUST OPENED WINDOWS. THERE ALSO WASN'T MUCH HEAT IN THE WINTER EITHER.

WE TOOK THE 63RD STREET CAR TO WESTERN AVENUE, THEN TRANSFERRED TO THE NORTH BOUND WESTERN AVE. CAR THAT WENT RIGHT PAST THE PARK AT BEMOUNT AVE. WE PASSED THROUGH CHINA TOWN ON THE WAY AND THAT WAS INTERESTING TO SEE. WHEN WE FINALLY PULLED UP IN FRONT OF THE BIG BEAUTIFUL GATES OF RIVERVIEW PARK, IT MADE THE WHOLE HOT UNCOMFORTABLE RIDE WELL WORTH IT.

WE COULDN'T WAIT TO GET INSIDE THE PARK. WE HAD ALL BEEN ABOUT HALF ASLEEP ON THE STREECAR RIDE. NOW WE WERE WIDE AWAKE AND BUMPING AND SHOVING EACH OTHER TO GET OFF THE CAR AND GET INSIDE THE PARK, WE WERE HIGH WITH EXCITEMENT. WHEN WE DID GET INSIDE THE PARK WE JUST STOOD THERE LOOKING AROUND, NOT KNOWING WHERE TO START OR WHICH WAY TO GO. BOB HAD BEEN TO THE PARK BEFORE AND SUGGESTED THAT WE COULD TAKE A RIDE ON THE LITTLE STEAM ENGINE TRAIN THAT CIRCLED THE PARK AND WE COULD SEE WHERE EVERYTHING WAS.

IT SOUNDED LIKE A GOOD PLACE TO START SO WE TOOK THE TRAIN RIDE. IT WAS VERY RELAXING AND COOLED US DOWN SOMEWHAT. AFTER THE TRAIN RIDE WE FOUND A REFRESHMENT AREA AND SAT DOWN AT A TABLE TO EAT WHAT WAS LEFT OF OUR LUNCHES. THE ROOTBEER AT THE FOOD STAND WAS FIVE CENTS A GLASS. I HELD UP A QUARTER AND SAID, I FOUND THIS A COUPLE OF WEEKS AGO AND THE ROOTBEER IS ON ME. WE KINDA WOLFED DOWN OUR LUNCHES PRETTY FAST AND SET OFF ON OUR LONG DAY OF ADVENTURE, AND WHAT A DAY IT WAS. RIDING HOME THAT EVENING WE WERE A BUNCH OF TIRED, SUN-BURNED CONTENTED GUYS. I THINK THAT SPECIAL DAY KINDA CEMENTED OUR FRIENDSHIPS WITH ONE ANOTHER THAT LASTED OUR ENTIRE LIVES......

THE ICE POND

WHEN I WAS A BOY GROWING UP DURING THE 1930S, OUR COMMUNITY LAY ON THE FRINGE OF CHICAGO, ILLINOIS. THE AREA THAT WE LIVED IN WAS MORE LIKE A SMALL TOWN THEN A PART OF CHICAGO AND WAS CALLED CLEARING. THERE WERE MORE THEN A HUNDRED FACTORIES IN THE AREA. PEOPLE TRIED TO LIVE CLOSE TO THERE WORK PLACE SO THAT THEY COULD WALK TO WORK. THERE WEREN'T MANY AUTOMOBILES IN A WORKING CLASS NEIGHBORHOOD LIKE OURS. CLEARING WAS A FRIENDLY PLACE.

ALTHOUGH IT WAS RUMORED THAT SOME OF AL CAPONES MEN USED CLEARING FOR HIDING OUT FROM TIME TO TIME, I NEVER SAW ANYONE THAT LOOKED LIKE A GANGSTER TO ME.

CLEARING WAS KNOWN THROUGHOUT THE SOUTHWEST SIDE OF THE CITY FOR ITS GOOD ATHLETES AND ITS PRETTY GIRLS. IT WAS NICE TO BE A PART OF IT AND A GOOD PLACE TO LIVE AND GROW UP IN. IN THE SUMMER, JUST ABOUT EVERYONE UP TO MIDDLE AGE PLAYED SOFTBALL. IT WAS AN EASY GAME TO PLAY, WITH A LOT OF

ACTION AND IT DIDN'T REQUIRE A LOT OF EQUIPMENT. THERE WERE INDUSTRIAL AND BUSINESS SOFTBALL LEAGUES THAT PLAYED EVERY WEEK NIGHT NIGHT, AND THERE WERE ALSO TWO HARDBALL BASEBALL TEAMS IN THE NEIGHBORHOOD AND THEY BOTH WERE ALWAYS PRETTY GOOD. THERE WAS MORE VACANT PROPERTY THEN THERE WERE HOMES, SO THERE WERE MANY BALL DIAMONDS SCATTERED ALL OVER TOWN. SOME OF THESE FIELDS WOULD BE FLOODED IN THE WINTER AND TURNED INTO ICE SKATING RINKS. WE CALLED THEM ICE PONDS.

IN THE LATE FALL SOME OF US BOYS WOULD GO OVER TO MR. VAN ARCOS FARM AND ASK HIM IF HE'D PLOW A TRENCH AROUND THE VACANT FIELD AT 62ND AND MASSISOIT AVE. HE'D ALWAYS LOOK AT US AND LAUGH AND SAY, RUN ALONG BOYS, I'M BUSY. BUT IN THE NEXT DAY OR TWO HE'D BE THERE BRIGHT AND EARLY, WITH HIS TEAM OF HORSES AND PLOW AND DO THE JOB. AFTER HE HAD FINISHED, HE'D ALWAYS SAY, I'LL PUT IT ON YOUR BILL. THERE NEVER WAS A BILL. MR. VAN ARCO WAS THE LAST FARMER IN OUR AREA, MAYBE THE LAST FARMER IN CHICAGO. HIS FARM IS NOW PART OF MIDWAY AIRPORT. HE ALSO DUG BASEMENTS WITH HIS TEAM OF HORSES. HE USED A SPECIAL SCOOP FOR THAT. HE WAS ALSO THE LOCAL GARBAGE COLLECTOR. HE'D GO DOWN THE ALLEYS WITH HIS HORSES AND WAGON AND SCOOP UP THE GARBAGE THAT WAS PILED IN CERTAIN PLACES AND THROW IT INTO HIS WAGON WITH A BIG SHOVEL.

WE DIDN'T HAVE GARBAGE CANS IN THOSE DAYS. MR. VAN ARCO PLAYED AN IMPORTANT ROLE BACK THEN.

AFTER THE FIELD WAS TRENCHED, SOME OF US BOYS WOULD GO OVER TO THE FIRE STATION AND ASK THE FIREMEN IF THEY WOULD FLOOD THE FIELD FOR US. THEY'D ALWAYS SAY, SINCE YOU BOYS ARE SO POLITE IN ASKING, YES, WE'LL FLOOD IT WHEN THE TIME IS RIGHT. THOSE FIREMEN WOULD HAVE MADE GREAT WEATHERMEN FOR THEY ALWAYS SEEMED TO KNOW EXACTLY WHEN TO FLOOD THE POND.

OUR POND WAS THE LARGEST IN TOWN. IT TOOK ALL NIGHT TO FLOOD IT USING FIREHOSES THAT WERE TURNED ON FULL AT EACH END OF THE FIELD. THE ICE POND WASN'T READY TO BE USED YET. THEY WOULD LET THE ICE SETTLE INTO THE GROUND FOR A COUPLE OF DAYS AND THEN REFLOOD IT. NOW IT WAS READY FOR A LONG WINTER OF FUN. THERE WAS A HOCKEY RINK LAID OUR ON THE POND TO BE USED DURING THE DAYTIME HOURS. AFTER SIX O'CLOCK IN THE EVENING THE ICE WAS FOR PLEASURE SKATING ONLY. EVERYONE TOOK THEIR PLEASURE IN THEIR OWN WAY. SOME WOULD DO FANCY SKATING WITH SPINS AND JUMPS. SOME WOULD ICE DANCE, WHILE OTHERS WOULD HOLD HANDS AND SKATE AROUND THE POND. MY BUNCH WERE PRETTY GOOD SKATERS, BOTH FORWARD AND BACK AND COULD DO SOME TURNS AND JUMPS, BUT WE MOSTLY LIKED TO SKATE HARD AND FAST.

SOMETIMES THERE WOULD BE A DAISY CHAIN FORMED WITH PERHAPS FIFTEEN OR TWENTY PEOPLE. THEY'D LINE UP IN A ROW ONE BEHIND ANOTHER AND TAKE HOLD OF THE WAIST IN FRONT OF THEM WITH BOTH HANDS AND SKATE THAT WAY. THE WHOLE THING LOOKED TO ME LIKE A BIG LONG SNAKE WIGGLING AROUND THE POND.

MOST PEOPLE HEATED THEIR HOMES WITH COAL FURNACES BACK THEN. SCRAP WOOD, BROKEN TREE LIMBS AND ANY OTHER JUNK WOOD WOULD BE SAVED DURING THE YEAR, JUST FOR THE ICE SKATING SEASON. THERE WAS ALMOST ALWAYS A BONFIRE AT THE POND. SOMETIMES SMALL AND SOMETIMES LARGE, IT DEPENDED ON THE WEATHER AND HOW MANY PEOPLE WERE THERE AT THE TIME. SOME PEOPLE WOULD BRING SLEDS AND PULL THERE CHILDREN OR EACH OTHER AROUND THE OUTSIDE EDGES OF THE POND. THERE WERE SEVERAL LOGS, SOME SMALL BARRELS AND WOODEN BOXES PLACES AROUND THE FIRE AREA SO THAT SKATERS COULD CHANGE INTO THEIR SKATES AND LATER BACK INTO THEIR DHOES. ALSO PEOPLE COULD REST AND WARM THEMSELVES BY THE FIRE.

AN ODD THING HAPPENED TO ME ONE WINTER EVENING. IT WAS REALLY QUITE SIMPLE, YET UNREAL. IT WAS ABOUT EIGHT THIRTY IN THE EVENING AND MOST OF THE SKATERS HAD ALREADY GONE HOME AS IT HAD BEEN SNOWING FOR ABOUT AN HOUR. IT WAS A QUIET NIGHT AND THE BIG SNOWFLAKES JUST KINDA FLOATED

DOWN AND QUICKLY COVERED THE GROUND AND ICE. I
HAD DECIDED TO SKATE AROUND THE POND ONE MORE
TIME AND WHEN I GOT TO THE OTHER END OF THE
POND I STOPPED AND TURNED AROUND. LOOKING BACK
AT THE FIRE I COULD SEE THE LAST OF THE SKATERS
MOVING ABOUT, PREPARING TO LEAVE. ALTHOUGH
THE FIRE HAD BEEN A BIG ONE THAT NIGHT, FROM
WHERE I WAS, IT NOW LOOKED SMALL AND FLICKERING
THROUGH THE FALLING SNOW. IT WAS ORANGE YELLOW
COLORED AND LOOKED TO ME LIKE A SPUTTERING
CANDLE FLAME. I GLANCED OVER AT THE NEAREST
STREETLIGHT AND THOUGH IT'S BRIGHT LIGHT SHONE
THROUGH THE SNOW, IT SEEMED TO BE TWINKLING
LIKE A STAR AND MADE THE FALLING SNOWFLAKES
SPARKLE AND SHINE. THERE WAS AN ALMOST FULL
MOON AND AS I LOOKED UP AT IT, IT REMINDED ME OF
A GREAT WHITE SNOWBALL, IT SEEMED SO CLOSE. IT
LIT UP THE SNOW ON THE GROUND AND GAVE ME THE
FEELING OF BEING IN A DAY-NIGHT PLACE. I WATCHED
THE HUGE SNOWFLAKES FLOATING DOWN AND FELT
THEM GENTLY LANDING ON MY UPTURNED FACE. IT
WAS AS THOUGH I WAS STANDING ALL ALONE IN A PLACE
I DIDN'T KNOW. A WONDERLAND.

THE WORLD, MY WORLD WAS CALM AND SERENE AND
SO QUET AND STILL TO THIS DAY, WHENEVER I THINK
ABOUT THOSE FEW MOMENTS THAT HAPPENED TO ME
SO MANY, MANY YEARS AGO, I GET A WARM FEELING OF
COMPLETE PEACE.

A FEW DAYS AFTER CHRISTMAS, PEOPLE WOULD BEGIN TO BRING THEIR USED CHRISTMAS TREES OVER TO THE POND. MEN AND THE BIGGER BOYS WOULD THEN START TO ARRANGE THEM INTO A PILE IN THE MIDDLE OF THE ICE POND. THE PILE KEPT GROWING DAY BY DAY. WHEN THE FIRST SATURDAY AFTER NEW YEARS CAME, THE PILE WAS ABOUT AS HIGH AS A HOUSE. THAT WOULD BE THE SPECIAL DAY, OR ACTUALLY NIGHT. CROWDS OF PEOPLE, AT LEAST HALF THE NEIGHBORHOOD CAME TO THE POND THAT EVENING.

THE NEIGHBORHOOD POLICE, WE HAD ONLY TWO OF THEM, WERE THERE EARLY AND DOING THEIR JOB. THEY POSITIONED THE PEOPLE AROUND THE PILE OF TREES, FAR ENOUGH BACK SO THAT THEY'D BE SAFE. ALL THE AREA FIREMEN WERE ALSO THERE WITH THEIR FIRE TRUCK AND THEIR HOSES CONNECTED UP TO THE CITY FIRE HYDRANTS AND READY TO GO IN CASE THEY WERE NEEDED. THEY'D SUPERVISE THE PROCEEDINGS. WHEN IT WAS COMPLETELY DARK, THE PILE OF TREES WAS SET ON FIRE AT SEVERAL POINTS. THE VERY DRY PINE AND FIR TREES FLARED UP IN DRAMATIC FASHION. IT WAS A SIGHT TO SEE. THE FIRE BECAME A FIERCE INFERNO ALMOST IMMEDIATELY. IT POPPED AND CRACKLED AND RAGED AND SNAPPED AND THREW SPARKS AND CLOUDS OF SMOKE AND FIRE HIGH INTO THE SKY, LIGHTING UP THE ENTIRE AREA. WITHIN AN HOUR THE FIRE WAS ALMOST OUT, LEAVING JUST A HEAP OF GLOWING EMBERS. THE FIREMEN TURNED THEIR HOSES ON WHAT WAS LEFT OF THE FIRE AND WASHED IT ALL AWAY.

THE BURNING OF THE TREES MARKED THE END OF THE HOLIDAY SEASON. IT WAS BACK TO SCHOOL FOR THE CHILDREN AND A LONG WINTER AHEAD: WE KNEW THAT WE WERE IN FOR A LOT OF SKATING AND WINTER FUN. WHEN I LOOK BACK AT THOSE LONG AGO DEPRESSION DAYS THAT I GREW UP IN, I DON'T REMEMBER BEING POOR. ALMOST EVERYBODY I KNEW WAS IN THE SAME BOAT THAT WE WERE IN. WE WERE KIDS GROWING UP AND HAPPY TO HAVE FRIENDS AND OTHER GOOD PEOPLE AROUND US. IT WAS A GREAT TIME AND PLACE FOR GROWING UP. WE LEARNED THE VALUE OF MONEY, OF FRIENDSHIPS THAT HAVE LASTED A LIFE TIME, AND THE VALUE OF RESPECT FOR OTHER PEOPLE, BOTH YOUNG AND OLD. THROUGH THE YEARS, I'VE SECRETLY THOUGHT OF THE NEIGHBORHOOD OF CLEARING AS BEING A SORT OF CAMELOT. IT ONCE WAS... BUT IS NO MORE... AT LEAST, NOT AS I REMEMBER IT......

SUMMER SCHOOL

GEOMETRY WAS AND IS ONE OF THE DEEP DARK MYSTERIES OF LIFE TO ME. I CAN'T THINK OF WHY IT WAS EVER INVENTED. WHAT GOOD WOULD IT BE TO A GUY THAT WAS GOING TO WORK AT BEING A BUTCHER, A CAB DRIVER OR AN AIRPLANE PILOT, A POLICEMAN, A FIREMAN OR A GIRL BEING A TYPIST OR A HOUSEWIFE? THE ONLY REASON I CAN FIGURE FOR ANYONE TO TAKE INTEREST IN IT AT ALL IS IF THEY WANTED TO BE A GEOMETRY TEACHER. THEY COULD SIT UP AT A DESK IN FRONT OF A BUNCH OF BEWILDERED STUDENTS AND WITHHOLD THE MYSTERIES OF GEOMETRY FROM THEM.

I SAT THROUGH THE FALL SEMESTER OF BEGINNER GEOMETRY AND FLUNKED. I NEVER CAUGHT ON TO THE BASIC CONCEPTS OF WHAT IT WAS ABOUT OR WHY EVERYBODY WAS REQUIRED TO TAKE IT. THE NEXT SEMESTER I SAT THROUGH THE SAME CLASS, SAME TEACHER, DIFFERENT FELLOW STUDENTS AND BARELY SKINNED BY. I STILL DIDN'T UNDERSTAND MOST OF IT. THEY EVEN GAVE ME SPECIAL COUNCILING, IT REALLY DIDN'T HELP MUCH.

I STILL NEEDED GEOMETRY TWO TO GRADUATE AND THE ONLY WAY I COULD FIGURE TO GET IT WAS BY GOING TO SUMMER SCHOOL. I DECIDED TO TAKE TWO CLASSES AS LONG AS I WAS GOING ANYWAY. THE CREDIT I'D GET FOR THE SECOND SUBJECT WOULD ACT LIKE A SAETY NET FOR ME IN CASE I EVER GOT INTO TROUBLE WITH ANOTHER CLASS. ENGLISH WAS ALWAYS ONE OF MY EASIER SUBJECTS SO THAT WOULD BE MY NUMBER TWO CLASS. I WENT AHEAD AND SURRENDERED MYSELF TO SUMMER SCHOOL. I TRIED TO STAY FOCUSED AND PAID SHARP ATTENTION IN GEOMETRY CLASS. I HAD TO, THERE STILL WASN'T MUCH OF IT GETTING THROUGH TO ME.

MY ENGLISH CLASS WAS AT ELEVEN O'CLOCK. IT SEEMED TO ME THAT WE WERE SITTING IN A WARMING OVEN AT OUR DESKS. THE WINDOWS WERE OPEN AND WE COULD HEAR STREET NOISES BUT THERE WAS NO AIR CONDITIONING IN 1940. MY HEAD WAS NODDING BACK AND FORTH LIKE A PENDULUM OF A HALL CLOCK.

THERE WERE ABOUT TWELVE BOYS AND TWO GIRLS IN THE ENGLISH CLASS AND IT SEEMED THAT HALF THE CLASS WOULD NOD FOR A WHILE AND THEN THE OTHER HALF WOULD TAKE THEIR TURN AT IT.

THE KINDLY LITTLE OLD LADY THAT WAS OUR TEACHER NEVER SEEMED TO NOTICE OUR NODDINGS. SHE MOSTLY READ POETRY FROM A SMALL BOOK. ONCE IN A WHILE SHE'D PAUSE AND LOOK UP FROM HER BOOK AND ASK US

IF WE UNDERSTOOD THE PASSAGE THAT SHE HAD JUST READ. WELL, HALF OF US WOULD BE NODDING, SO I GUESS THAT SHE TOOK THE NODDING AS A YES AND SHE'D GO BACK TO HER READING. SHE NEVER ASKED ANY OF US A DIRECT QUESTION. MY GUESS IS THAT SHE HAD DONE MANY SUMMER SCHOOLS BEFORE AND SHE FIGURED THAT IF WE WERE WILLING TO SIT THROUGH THE HEAT OF SUMMER, WE WERE TRYING AND DESERVED TO PASS. NO ONE IN THE CLASS FAILED. MOST KIDS WERE ONLY TAKING ONE CLASS SO THERE WEREN'T ANY LUNCH BREAKS. THERE WAS A FIFTEEN MINUTE SPACE BETWEEN CLASSES SO I WENT OUT THE FRONT DOORS BETWEEN CLASSES AND SAT ON THE STEPS IN THE SHADE.

A BOY OF ABOUT MY AGE WALKED OVER AND SAT NEXT TO ME AND SAID, HI. I LOOKED AT HIM AND COULDN'T BELIEVE MY EYES. AS HOT AS IT WAS, HE WAS WEARING A SUIT AND TIE AND HIS HAIR WAS NEATLY CUT AND HIS SHOES SHINED. I FIGURED THAT HE MUST HAVE A JOB IN A BANK OR SOMETHING LIKE THAT AFTER CLASSES TO BE DRESSED SO. HE TOLD ME THAT HIS NAME WAS JACK AND HE PULLED OUT A PACK OF CIGARETTES FROM HIS SHIRT POCKET AND OFFERED ME ONE.

I TOLD HIM MY NAME AND DECLINED HIS OFFER. THE ONLY EXPERIENCE I'D EVER HAD WITH SMOKING WAS WHEN I WAS EIGHT YEARS OLD. A PAL OF MINE BROUGHT TWO CIGARETTES FROM HOME AND WE HID BETWEEN TWO GARAGES OUT IN THE ALLEY TO TRY SMOKING THEM. AFTER HAVING A HARD TIME LIGHTING THEM,

WE BOTH TOOK THREE OR FOUR PUFFS OF THEM AND THREW THEM AWAY. IT WASN'T THE FUN THAT WE THOUGHT IT WOULD BE AND THE TASTE WAS TERRIBLE. JACK AND I TALKED ABOUT THE USUAL THINGS THAT TEENAGERS TALK ABOUT, SPORTS, MUSIC AND GIRLS. HE SEEMED TO BE A REGULAR GUY BUT I STILL WONDERED, WHY THE SUIT? I THOUGHT IT WAS AGAINST SCHOOL RULES TO SMOKE WITHIN A BLOCK OF THE SCHOOL, BUT JACK KEPT SMOKING EVERY DAY AND NOBODY EVER QUESTIONED HIM ABOUT IT. MAYBE IT DIDN'T COUNT IN SUMMER SCHOOL.

ON FRIDAY JACK ASKED ME WHAT I DID WITH MY SATURDAY NIGHTS. I TOLD HIM THAT IF I DIDN'T HAVE A DATE, I'D HANG OUT WITH THE GUYS FROM MY NEIGHBORHOOD, MAYBE SHOOT SOME POOL OR TAKE IN A MOVIE.

HE SAID, I LIVE IN THE OGDEN PARK AREA. THERE'S A PRETTY GOOD CROWD THAT HANGS OUT AROUND 63RD AND ASHLAND AVENUE. WHY DON'T YOU COME OVER THERE ABOUT SEVEN OR SO TOMORROW NIGHT IF YOU'RE NOT DOING ANYTHING AND WE'LL FIGURE OUT SOMETHING. WELL, IT WAS SATURDAY NIGHT AND THERE WEREN'T ANY OF MY PALS AROUND SO ABOUT 6:30 I HOPPED ON A STREETCAR AND WAS OFF FOR ASHLAND AVE. AS THE STREETCAR WAS PASSING THE OGDEN THEATER, BEFORE THE STOP AT ASHLAND AVENUE, I SAW JACK STANDING THERE TALKING TO TWO GIRLS AND A GUY. WHEN I WALKED UP TO THEM JACK

SAID, HEY! YOU MADE IT AND HE INTRODUCED ME TO TOM, ALICE AND PATTIE.

ABOUT THAT TIME A TALL SKINNY KID WALKED UP TO US, HE LOOKED A LITTLE OLDER THAN THE REST OF US. JACK INTRODUCED ME TO SLIM. SLIM GAVE ME A QUICK GLANCE AND SAID HI. THEN HE LOOKED BACK AT JACK AND SAID, I FOUND ONE.

JACK SAID O.K., AND SAID TO THE REST OF US, LET'S TAKE A WALK, AND TO ME HE SAID, COME ON BUD, WALK WITH ME.

WE WALKED TO THE FIRST CORNER WEST AND TURNED INTO A NEIGHBORHOOD STREET. SLIM WAS LEADING THE WAY. THE STREET WAS LINED WITH PARKED CARS, THOSE OF MOVIE GOERS I FIGURED. WE CONTINUED DOWN THE STREET FOR ABOUT THREE QUARTERS OF A BLOCK.

SLIM IN THE LEAD WALKED OVER TO AN ALMOST NEW BUICK AND GOT INTO THE DRIVERS SIDE AND UNLOCKED ALL OF THE DOORS OF THE CAR. JACK OPENED THE BACK DOOR AND TOLD ME TO GET IN. NEXT CAME ALICE AND THEN JACK GOT IN HIMSELF. TOM AND PATTIE GOT IN THE FRONT SEAT ALONG SIDE OF SLIM. SLIM WAS GOING TO DRIVE AND HE WAS TAKING A LONG TIME TO TURN ON THE LIGHTS AND GET THE CARE STARTED. I GUESSED THAT HE WASN'T TOO FAMILIAR WITH HIS DADS NEW CARE YET. HE DROVE THE CARE OVER TO ASHLAND AVE.

AND THEN TURNED SOUTH. IT LOOKED LIKE WE WERE HEADING FOR THE SUBURBS. AS SOON AS WE GOT ONTO ASHLAND, PATTIE AND TOM STARTED HUGGING AND KISSING AND WHENEVER WE HAD TO STOP AT A RED LIGHT, PATTIE WOULD TURN TO SLIM AND THEY WOULD HUG AND KISS. ONE TIME WE SAT THROUGH TWO RED LIGHTS WHILE THEY WENT AT IT. IN THE MEANTIME JACK AND ALICE WERE DOING THAT SAME THING IN THE BACK SEAT. AFTER ONE BREAK JACK LEANED OVER ALICE AND ASKED ME IF I WANTED TO HAVE A GO WITH ALICE. I SAID NO, I'M KINDA TIRED, I THINK I'LL JUST SIT BACK AND RELAX FOR A TIME.

ALICE DIDN'T SEEM TO TAKE OFFENSE AT ME DECLINGING. SHE WAS SO BUSY WITH JACK THAT I DON'T THINK SHE EVEN NOTICED OR REMEMBERED THAT I WAS THERE.

WE HAD BEEN DRIVING AROUND FOR MORE THEN AN HOUR WHEN JACK, LOOKING AT HIS WATCH SAID, I THINK THAT WE BETTER BE GETTING BACK. ON THE RETURN TRIP THE SAME ACTIVITIES CONTINUED IN THE CAR. IT OCCURRED TO ME THAT SOMETHING WAS WRONG. WHY DID WE HAVE TO DRIVE AROUND? WHY COULDN'T THEY HAVE DONE WHAT THEY WERE DOING IN THE CAR WHERE IT HAD BEEN PARKED, IN THE FIRST PLACE?

WHEN WE GOT BACK TO THE SIDE STREET NEXT TO THE THEATER IT WAS STILL PACKED WITH PARKED CARS. WE HAD TO GO DOWN THE STREET AN ADDITIONAL BLOCK

BEFORE WE FOUND A PLACE TO PARK. WE CLOSED THE
WINDOWS AND GOT OUT OF THE CAR, BUT NOBODY
BOTHERED TO LOCK THE DOORS. WE WALKED BACK UP
TO 63ᴿᴰ STREET AND I THOUGHT THAT IT WAS KINDA
FUNNY THAT SLIM WOULD LEAVE AN ALMOST NEW
CAR UNCLOCKED AND PARKED ON A CLUTTER STREET
WHEN WE WERE GOING UP TO 63ᴿᴰ.

WE ALL WENT INTO A GREAT BIG ICE-CREAM SHOP AND
OUR CAR PALS DISPERSED IN THE SHOP AND MINGLED
WITH OTHER KIDS. THE SHOP MUST HAVE BEEN THE
HANDGOUT PLACE FOR TEENAGERS IN THE AREA
BECAUSE THERE WERE PLENTY OF THEM THERE.

JACK AND I SAT AT A SMALL TABLE AND ORDERED
BANANA SPLITS AND JACK ASKED ME WHAT I THOUGHT
OF HIS GANG.

I ANSWERED THAT THEY WERE A FRIENDLY BUNCH.
WHAT I REALLY THOUGHT WAS THAT THEY WERE A LOT
MORE HARD-SHELLED AND MATURE THAN ANYONE
THAT I HUNG AROUND WITH, BUT I DIDN'T TELL JACK
THAT.

YEAH, HE LAUGHED, ESPECIALLY THE GIRLS. THEN HE
ASKED ME IF I'D LIKE TO DO ANYTHING ELSE AND ADDED
THAT HE HAD AN USHER BUDDY THAT CAN GET US INTO
THE OGDEN THEATER BY THE SIDE DOOR FOR FREE.

I SAID, NO THANKS JACK, I'M GOING FISHING WITH SOME FRIENDS IN THE MORNING AND I WANT TO GET UP EARLY, I THINK I'LL CALL IT A DAY. MONDAY WAS ANOTHER SCORCHING HOT DAY. AND WHY NOT, IT WAS THE MIDDLE OF JULY IN CHICAGO.

JACK AND I MET BETWEEN CLASSES AND I SAID TO HIM, SLIM HAD SOME TROUBLE GETTING GOING THE OTHER NIGHT. I GUESS HE'S NOT USE TO HIS DADS NEW CAR YET.

JACK LOOKED AT ME IN A FUNNY WAY AND SAID, SLIMS DAD DOESN'T OWN A CAR.

WITH A LITTLE FROWN ON MY FACE I ASKED, THEN WHOSE CAR WAS IT. JACK ANSWERED, I DON'T KNOW. WE LOOK FOR A CAR WITH THE KEYS IN IT AND TAKE IT FOR A RIDE. YOU WOULDN'T BELIEVE HOW MANY PEOPLE FORGET THEIR KEYS. I THOUGHT YOU KNEW THAT WE WERE ON A JOY RIDE.

JACKS REPLY HIT ME LIKE A TON OF BRICKS. WHEN I THOUGHT BACK TO THAT NIGHT, THE WHOLE THING WAS SO OBVIOUS. I WOULD HAVE MADE A CRACKERJACK OF A DETECTIVE, BEING AS DUMB AS I SEEMED TO BE. NAÏVE IS A KINDER WORD.

NO I DIDN'T KNOW I SAID, WHAT IF WE GOT CAUGHT?

NOTHING MUCH JACK REPLIED, WE'RE TEENAGERS. THEY TAKE US TO THE POLICE STATION AND PUT US

EACH IN DIFFERENT ROOMS. I GUESS THEY THINK THAT WE'LL GET SCARED ENOUGH BEING ALONE FOR A WHILE THAT WE WON'T DO IT AGAIN. THEY DON'T KNOW MY GANG. WE'VE BEEN THROUGH IT SO MANY TIMES THAT IT DOESN'T BOTHER US A BIT. AFTER ABOUT AN HOUR THEY CALL OUR PARENTS, GIVE US A LITTLE LECTURE AND SEND US HOME THINKING THAT OUR FOLKS WILL LAY THE LAW DOWN ON US. THEY DO, BUT IT JUST MAKES US MORE CAREFUL. WE'RE CAREFUL NOT TO MESS UP THE CARS. WE DO USE SOME OF THEIR GAS AND MAYBE PARK IN A DIFFERENT PLACE, BUT NO REAL HARMS EVER DONE. I GUESS NOT MANY COMPLAIN BACAUSE THERE'S NEVER ANY COPS AROUND. JACK LOOKED AT ME AND ASKED, HAVEN'T YOU EVER BEEN ARRESTED OR IN JAIL?

HECK NO I ANSWERED, HAVE YOU?

YEAH HE ANSWERED, A FEW TIMES. MOSTLY FOR STEALING IN STORES; HE SAID EVER SO MATTER OF FACTLY, LIKE IT WAS OK AND THE NORMAL THING TO DO. HE WENT ON, SLIM AND I JUST GOT BACK FROM DOING FOUR MONTHS IN ST. CHARLES FOR STEALING. WE'RE GONNA HAVE TO BE MORE CAREFUL FROM NOW ON. THE NEXT TIME WE GET CAUGHT, THE STRETCH WILL BE FOR A YEAR. HE WENT ON SOME MORE, THAT'S WHY I'M TAKING TWO SUBJECTS NOW. NEXT SUMMER I'LL TAKE TWO MORE AND BE RIGHT BACK WHERE I BELONG. I DRESS LIKE I DO IN SCHOOL BECAUSE I'M ON GOOD BEHAVIOR I KNEW WHAT ST. CHARLES WAS. IT WAS A HOME FOR WAYWARD AND DELINQUENT BOYS. MY

CAR PALS WERE ON A PATH THAT I CERTAINLY DIDN'T WANT TO TRAVEL.

JACK AND I REMAINED FRIENDLY AT SCHOOL FOR THE REST OF THE SUMMER SCHOOL BUT THAT'S WHERE OUR FRIENDSHIP ENDED. WE NEVER SAW EACH OTHER AWAY FROM SCHOOL PROPERTY AGAIN.

MY GRADES CAME IN THE MAIL AND I WAS SURPRISED AT THE HIGH GRADE I RECEIVED IN ENGLISH. I SKINNED BY IN GEOMETRY AND PROMPLY FORGOT WHAT LITTLE I HAD LEARNED ABOUT IT.

IT HAD BEEN A PRETTY DULL SUMMER, BUT IT WASN'T A COMPLETE WASTE. I EARNED TWO GRADES AND I LEARNED SOME THINGS ABOUT PEOPLE AND LIFE THAT THEY DON'T TEACH IN SUMMER SCHOOL......

COURTESY WITH DIGNITY

OLD BILL AND I WERE PUT TOGETHER AS A TEAM BY THE MANAGER OF THE RESTAURANT THAT WE BOTH WORKED FOR. WE WERE CALLED MUTT AND JEFF BY OUR FELLOW WORKERS IN A GOOD NATURED WAY BECAUSE OF THE DIFFERENCE IN OUR SIZES. BILL WAS A STRAIGHT BACKED, QUIET OLD GENTLEMAN IN HIS SIXTIES AND WAS ABOUT SIX FEET TALL. I HAD JUST TURNED EIGHTEEN AND WAS A GOOD SIX INCHES SHORTER THAN BILL. I GUESS TOGETHER, WE WERE QUIT A FUNNY LOOKING PAIR.

AMERICA HAD BEEN FORCED INTO WORLD WAR TWO A FEW MONTHS EARLIER, WHILE I WAS STILL IN HIGH SCHOOL. THE COUNTRY WAS JUST COMING OUT OF THE BIG DEPRESSION AND IT WAS QUICKLY FOLLOWED BY INFLATION CLOSE ON ITS HEELS. A LOT OF OLDER RETIRED PEOPLE, INCLUDING BILL CAME OUT OF RETIREMENT TO SUPPLEMENT THEIR MEAGER PENSIONS AND ALSO TRY AND HELP WITH THE WAR EFFORT. I WAS A SHY AND SELF CONSCIOUS YOUNG MAN AND HAD A WAR DRAFT RATING OF 1-A. IN 1942, MY DRAFT CLASSIFICATION WAS KNOWN AS DRAFT BAIT AND I COULD BE CALLED UP TO SERVE AT ANY TIME. NO BUSINESS PEOPLE WANTED

TO BREAK IN SOMEONE THAT WOULD BE LEAVING FOR SERVICE ANY DAY SO I COULDN'T FIND A DECENT JOB. I HAD HIRED ON AT THE RESTAURANT FOR FIFTY CENTS AN HOUR AND WAS ALLOWED TO WORK TEN HOURS A DAY, SIX DAYS A WEEK, SIXTY HOURS AT STRAIGHT TIME BECAUSE OF THE SCARCITY OF HELP AVAILABLE. THIRTY DOLLARS A WEEK WAS NOT BAD AT THAT TIME. THE RESTRAURANT ORGANIZATION HAD CONTRACTED TO SUPPLY THE FOOD NEEDS OF THE CONSTRUCTION WORKERS, TRUCK DRIVERS AND ALL OTHER PEOPLE THAT WERE EMPLOYED TO BUILD AN ENORMOUS DEFENSE PLANT FOR THE FORD MOTOR COMPANY ON THE SOUTHWEST EDGE OF THE CITY OF CHICAGO, ILLINOIS.

THE JOKING AND JIBS THAT WERE DIRECTED AT BILL AND ME WERE MUTUALLY SHARED BY THE TWO OF US AND THAT MADE IT A LOT EASIER TO TAKE. IT KINDA BONDED US AS A TEAM. THE TRUTH WAS THAT NEITHER OF US WERE TRAINED OR EXPERIENCED OR EQUIPPED TO HANDLE THE JOB THAT WE WERE GIVEN. WE WERE ASSIGNED TO RUN A FOOD BUSINESS IN A LITTLE WOODEN SHACK CALLED A CANTEEN. THERE WERE SIX SUCH CANTEENS SCATTERED AROUND IN VARIOUS LOCATIONS ON THE SEVERAL HUNDRED ACRES OF MUDDY SWAMP AND LAND THAT WAS TO BE TRANSFORMED INTO A HUGE SPRAWLING DEFENSE COMPLEX. BILL AND I MUST HAVE PRESENTED QUITE A PATHETIC SIGHT TO THE ROUGH WORKMEN WHOSE

DIALY LIVES NATURALLY INCLUDE ARGUMENTS, FIGHTS, THREATS AND PROFANITY.

THE CANTEEN WAS ABOUT TEN FEET WIDE BY SIXTEEN FEET LONG AND HAD A DOOR AT EACH END OF THE BUILDING, WITH AN AISLE OF FOUR FEET IN WIDTH RUNNING FROM DOOR TO DOOR. THERE WAS A THREE FOOT FENCE THAT RAN ALONG THE AISLE TO SEPARATE OUR WORKING AREA FROM THE CUSTOMERS.

THE CUSTOMERS WERE TO FILE THROUGH THE BUILDING AND WE WOULD SERVE THEM IN A SEMBLANCE OF ORDER. THINGS DIDN'T WORK OUT QUITE THE WAY THE CANTEEN PLANNERS HAD ANTICIPATED. IN THE FIRST PLACE BILL AND I WERE TRYING TO SERVE THE WORKERS INDIVIDUALLY AND THAT PROVED TO BE TOO TIME CONSUMING. ALSO IN OUR LIMITED AMOUNT OF WORKING SPACE, BILL AND I SEEMED TO ALWAYS BE IN EACH OTHERS WAY. THE REAL PROBLEM WAS THAT WE ONLY HAD AN HOUR TO SERVE FROM TWO TO THREE HUNDRED MEN AND IT SOON WAS CLEAR THAT IT WAS AN IMPOSSIBLE TASK.

WE ASKED THE WORK FORMAN IF HE COULD DIVIDE SOME OF THE MENS LUNCH TIME BY HALF AN HOUR, WE DIDN'T MIND WORKING LONGER TO DO THE JOB RIGHT.

HE SAID THAT THERE WERE DIFFERENT MEN COMING AND GOING ALL THE TIME AND THERE WAS NO WAY THAT HE COULD WORK IT OUT. WHEN WE GOT BACK

TO THE BIG RESTAURANT AFTER THE LUNCH HOUR, WE TOLD THE RESTAURANT MANAGER ABOUT THE PROBLEM HE LOOKED AT US WITH KIND OF A BLANK STARE AND SAID IN A LEVEL TONE, JUST WORK IT OUT. EASY FOR HIM TO SAY, HE DIDN'T HAVE TO FACE THE HUNGRY AND VERY ANGRY MOB.

THE NEXT DAY BY THE TIME WE GOT TO THE MIDDLE OF THE LINE THERE WAS ALREADY GRUMBLING ABOUT THE SLOWNESS OF OUR SERVICE AND THE WAY IT CUT INTO THEIR LUNCH HOURS. AS THE LINE SLOWLY MOVED ALONG, THE GRUMBLING GOT WORSE AND WE HAD SOME COMPLAINTS DIRECTED AT US. IT SOON TURNED INTO DOWN RIGHT BROWBEATINGS, WITH A LOT OF CUSSING AND SWEARING. WHILE WAITING FOR OUR RIDE BACK TO THE RESTAURANT AFTER THE LUNCH HOUR. BILL AND I TALKED THE SITUATION OVER AND DECIDED THAT SOMETHING REMEDIAL HAD TO BE DONE QUICKLY OR THE CANTEEN PROBABLY WOULD BE TORN DOWN WITH US IN IT, AS ONE OF THE WORKERS HAD VERY VIVIDLY TOLD US. BILL AND I PUT OUR HEADS TOGETHER AND DECIDED ON A PLAN THAT AT THE TIME SEEMED DARING, DRASTIC AND WAS UNHEARD OF. I DON'T THINK THAT IT WAS THE FIRST SELF SERVICE OPERATION, BUT NEITHER OF US HAD EVER SEEN OR HEARD OF SUCH A THING. IT WAS THE ONLY WAY WE COULD THINK OF TO SPEED UP THE SERVICE AND ALSO MAYBE SAVE OUR NECKS. OUR PLAN WAS TO PUSH THE RACKS AND SHELVES IN OUR WORK AREA, THAT WE KEPT THE FOOD ON, RIGHT UP TO THE AISLE RAIL. ALL

THE FOOD, THE SANDWICHES, LITTLE PIES, CAKES AND OTHER THINGS WERE WRAPPED IN TRANSPARENT WAX PAPER AND LABELED WHAT EACH WAS AND THE PRICE. THE WORKMEN WOULD PICK OUT WHAT THEY WANTED AND PAY AT THE OUT DOOR WHERE THE COFFEE URNS WERE. I'D BE THE CASHIER AND BILL WOULD POUR OUT HE COFFEE AND RESTOCK THE RACKS, IF NEED BE. IT WOULD BE MUCH QUICKER THAN TRYING TO WAIT ON EACH MAN, ONE AT A TIME. THE OBVIOUS PROBLEM OF COURSE WOULD BE, IF SOME OF THE MEN WOULD SHOVE THINGS INTO THEIR POCKETS WHILE WALKING IN LINE. IF THIS HAPPENED, WE'D BE SHORT ON THE MONEY AT THE END OF THE LUNCH HOUR AND BILL AND I WOULD HAVE TO MAKE UP THE DIFFERENCE. WE COULD LOSE AS MUCH AS HALF A WEEKS SALARY IF IT WAS REALLY BAD, WE BOTH AGREED THAT IT WAS WORTH TRYING. I GOT HOLD OF THE WORK FORMAN IN THE BIG DINING ROOM THAT AFTERNOON AND TOLD HIM ABOUT OUR PLAN AND THAT WE WERE GOING TO TRY IT THE NEXT DAY.

HE LOOKED STRAIGHT AT ME FOR A LITTLE WHILE AND I GUESS THAT HIS CONSCIENCE WENT TO WORK A LITTLE BECAUSE HE SHOOK HIS HEAD AND TOLD ME THAT IT WOULDN'T WORK. THAT THE MEN WOULD STEAL US BLIND THE FIRST DAY.

I TOLD HIM THAT WE WERE GETTING SO MUCH GRIEF FROM THE MEN AND OUR BOSS THAT IF THIS PLAN DIDN'T WORK AND THE MEN DID STEAL FROM US, THAT WE'D

MAKE UP THE DIFFERENCE OUT OF OUR OWN POCKETS AND AT THE END OF THE DAY WE'D BOTH QUIT.

HE SHRUGGED AND TURNED TO LEAVE, THEN HE TURNED BACK, AND WITH A FROWN ON HIS FACE AND WHAT LOOKED LIKE A LITTLE EMBARESSMENT SAID, I'LL TALK TO THE MEN AND HE ADDED, KID, YOU TWO CHARACTERS ARE JUST TOO POLITE. YOU CAN'T DEAL WITH THESE CUT-THROATS BY SAYING PLEASE AND THANK YOU SIR AND STUFF LIKE THAT. THEY THINK YOU'RE A JOKE. YOU'VE GOT TO TREAT THEM LIKE THEY'RE USE TO AND CUSS A LITTLE YOUR SELVES IF YOU WANT TO GET ALONG WITH THEM.

BILL AND I GAVE QUITE A BIT OF THOUGHT AND DISCUSSION TO WHAT THE FOREMAN HAD SAID. IN OUR NAÏVE WAY OF THINKING WE BOTH WANTED TO BELIEVE THAT THE WORLD AND MOST OF ITS PEOPLE WERE BASICALLY HONEST. (I STILL THINK THAT WAY), AND SO WE WOULD GO THROUGH WITH THE PLAN AS SCHEDULED. I GUESS WE BOTH MUST HAVE HAD A LITTLE GAMBLING BLOOD IN OUR VEINS. NEITHER OF US COULD SEE ANYTHING WRONG WITH BEING POLITE, SO WE WOULD CONTINUE THAT PART IN A SOMEWHAT MODERATED VERSION.

THE NEXT DAY THE TRUCK THAT TOOK US AND OUR SUPPLIES TO THE CANTEEN WAS A FEW MINUTES LATE AND THE CONSTRUCTION WORKERS HAD ALREADY BEGUN TO FORM THE LINE OUTSIDE THE CANTEEN

DOOR. INSTEAD OF BEING ROUDY AND LOUD ABOUT THE DELAY THERE WAS A STRANGE QUIETNESS ABOUT THEM, SOMETHING LIKE THE CALM BEFORE THE STORM I THOUGHT. SOME OF THE WORKMEN HELPED US UPLOAD THE SUPPLIES FROM THE TRUCK AND CARRY THEM INSIDE THE CANTEEN, WHICH THEY HAD NEVER DONE BEFORE. IT SEEMED TO ME THAT THEY COULDN'T WAIT TO GET THEIR HANDS ON WHAT MIGHT TURN OUT TO BE A FREE LUNCH AT OUR EXPENSE.

THE WORK FORMAN MUST HAVE PASSED THE WORD AROUND ABOUT OUR NEW SETUP BECAUSE A FEW MINUTES LATER WHEN I OPENED THE FRONT DOOR WITH MORE THAN A FEW MISGIVINGS, THE WORK MEN BEGAN TO FILE THROUGH WITHOUT ASKING ANY QUESTIONS AS THOUGH IT WAS THE USUAL PROCEEDURE. BILL AND I WERE TOO BUSY TO WONDER WHY EVERYTING WAS GOING ALONG SO SMOOTHLY. WE HAD WORKED THROUGH ABOUT HALF THE LINE OF CUSTOMERS WHEN IT HAPPENED. I WAS WEARING A WHITE JACKET LIKE THOSE WORN BY BUSBOYS AND KITCHEN HELP. MY CASHBOX WAS SOMEWHAT LIKE A FISHING TACKEL BOX WITH A TRAY IN THE TOP IN WHICH I KEPT MY CHANGE IN SEPARATE LITTLE COMPARTMENTS AND I'D SLIP THE PAPER MONEY UNDER THE TRAY INTO THE BOTTOM OF THE BOX. IN MY HASTE TO KEEP THINGS GOING ALONG, I CAUGHT THE LOOSE SLEEVE OF MY JACKET ON THE CORNER OF THE CASHBOX AND SENT IT FLYING THROUGH THE AIR. IT LANDED UPSIDE DOWN ON THE OUTER SIDE OF MY COUNTER. BILL WAS BUSY

AT THE OTHER END OF THE BUILDING REPLACING MERCHANDISE AND THE MONEY WAS FLYING AND ROLLING AND BOUNCING ALL OVER THE PLACE. I WENT INTO A KIND OF SHOCK FOR A MOMENT AND DIDN'T HAVE TIME TO ACT OR THINK.

THE FIRST FOUR MEN IN THE LINE WENT INTO ALMOST IMMEDIATE ACTION, WHILE I STOOD FROZEN TO MY SPOT.

THE FIRST MAN SHUT THE OUT DOOR AND STOOD THERE WITH HIS BACK AGAINST IT. THE FOURTH MAN TURNED AROUND AND WITH HIS ARMS STRETCHED OUT, WOULDN'T LET THE MEN BEHIND HIM MOVE AHEAD. THE OTHER TWO MEN GOT DOWN ON THEIR HANDS AND KNEES AND WERE GRABBING MONEY OFF THE FLOOR WITH BOTH HANDS, AS FAST AS THEY COULD.

I STOOD THERE, ON MY SIDE OF THE COUNTER WITH MY MOUTH HALF OPENED, WATCHING THEM.

WHEN ONE OF THE MEN HAD HIS HANDS FULL HE LOOKED UP AT ME AND SAID, KID, WE DON'T KNOW HOW YOU ARRANGE YOUR DOUGH, SO WE'LL JUST THROW IT IN THE BOX AND YOU CAN SORT IT OUT YOURSELF, OK? MY ANSWER WAS A VERY WEAK OK.

AFTER THE LUNCH HOUR WAS OVER AND THE WORKMEN WERE GONE, BILL AND I DIDN'T TALK AT ALL WHILE WE WERE COUNTING THE CASH AND TAKING INVENTORY. WE HAD TIME TO DO IT TWICE. WE WERE BOTH

SURPRISED AND HAPPY TO SAY THE LEAST THAT OUR BOOKS HAD BALANCED PERFECTLY. THAT DAY WE HAD EARNED FAR MORE THAN OUR WAGES. IN SOME WAY, I KINDA THINK WITH THE HELP OF THE WORK FOREMAN, WE HAD MANAGED TO BREAK THROUGH THE SHELLS OF THIS BUNCH OF ROUGHNECKS THAT WE HAD BEEN SERVING. WE HAD A GIVEN THEM OUR SIMPLE HONESTY AND TRUST AND THEY HAD PAID US BACK IN KIND. WHAT I THINK WAS FAR MORE IMPORTANT WAS THAT WE HAD DEVELOPED A MUTUAL RESPECT WITH THEM. FROM THAT DAY ON WE GOT SOME YOUR WELCOME TO OUR THANK YOU AND SOME SMILES. A LOT OF HOW ARE YOU DOING TODAY AND OTHER SMALL TALK.

I LIKE TO THINK THAT OUR THANK YOU SIR HAD SOMETHING TO DO WITH THE OUTCOME. WHY NOT? A LITTLE COURTESY AND POLITENESS DOESN'T COST ANYTHING, AND GIVEN HONESTLY, THEY CAN ADD A LITTLE DIGNITY TO BOTH THE GIVER AND THE RECEIVER......

REWARD

REWARDS CAN BE LIKE SUPRISES, THEY CAN COME QUICKLY, UNEXPECTEDLY AND IN DIFFERENT SHAPES AND SIZES.

THE MAIN RESTAURANT OF THE CONSTRUCTON PROJECT WAS SOMEWHAT CENTERED IN THE MANY ACRES OF THE PROJECT AND WAS MADE OF WOOD AND WOULD BE TORN DOWN AFTER THE NINE BUILDINGS THAT WOULD BE THE HUGE DEFENSE PLANT WERE FINISHED. IT WAS OPEN FROM 6:30 AM TO 10:30 PM. THE EVENING SHIFT DID THE CLEAN UP WORK AND GOT THINGS READY FOR THE NEXT DAY. THE RESTAURANT HAD JUST ONE CLAIM TO FAME; IT HAD THE WORLDS LARGEST COFFEE URN. THE URN MADE 125 GALLONS OF COFFEE AT A TIME AND TOOK 39 POUNDS OF COFFEE AND TWO MEN TO DO THE JOB. THE RESTAURANT ORGANIZATION WAS ALSO INVOLVED IN THE CATERING BUSNESS. THEY CATERED WEDDINGS, BIRTHDAYS, ANNIVERSARIES AND ALL KINDS OF SPECIAL EVENTS.

PETE, THE RESTAURANTS SECOND CHEF HAD WORKED CATERING FOR YEARS AND WAS ASKED TO DO IT AGAIN.

HE WOULD BOSS THE CATERING JOBS AND HE ASKED ME IF I'D TRY WORKING ONE AND IF I LIKED THE WORK, MAYBE I WOULD BE HIS REGULAR ASSISTANT ON THE JOB. I SAID SURE, IT'D BE SOMETHING NEW AND I'D LIKE THE EXTRA MONEY. HE EXPLAINED TO ME ABOUT SETTING UP. HOW I WAS TO DRESS AND ACT WHILE WORKING THE AFFAIRS AND THE IMPORTANCE OF CLEANING UP AND MOVING OUT QUICKLY AFTER AN AFFAIR.

THE FIRST PARTY THAT I WORKED WAS KINDA HARD FOR ME. I HAD TO SMILE AND NOD AND BE POLITE AND SAY THANK YOU TO SOME VERY RUDE AND OBNOXIOUS PEOPLE.

PETE SAW MY DISCOMFORT AND PULLED ME ASIDE AND TOLD ME THAT THIS ISN'T PERSONAL, THIS IS THE WAY THAT SOME PEOPLE ARE. THEY'RE NOT OUR TYPE OF PEOPLE AND SO TO US THEY'RE NOT REAL. WE'RE HERE TO DO A JOB, THAT'S ALL.

I NEEDED FOR PETE TO SAY THAT. IT PUT THINGS INTO PERSPECTIVE FOR ME. I LEARNED SOME THINGS ON THAT FIRST JOB THAT HAVE STUCK WITH ME FOR EVER. FIRST, SOMETHING I HAD TO BE I WASN'T, AND ACTOR, AND SECONDALY, HOW TO HANDLE PEOPLE AND HAPPENINGS THAT WERE DIFFERENT FROM ME AND HOW I LIVED.

PETE WAS SMART AND I WENT ALONG WITH HIM WHENEVER HE ASK ME. WE CATERED EVENTS ALMOST

EVERY WEEK. SOME WERE SMALL AND INTIMATE WHILE OTHERS WERE LARGE AND NOISY.

IT WAS HARD WORK BUT I ENJOYED IT. SOME TIMES THE TIPS WERE REALLY GENEROUS.

THE BIGGEST EVENT WE CATERED THAT YEAR WAS THE BOB HOPE ALL-AMERICAN GOLF CLASSIC. IT WAS A CHARITY EVENT AND WAS HELD IN WESTMOUNT, ILLINOIS. A PROMINENT CHICAGO SUBURB. IT WAS A TRUE GALA AFFAIR ATTENDED BY MULITUDES OF PEOPLE THAT INCLUDED THE RICH AND FAMOUS. THERE WAS A LOT OF ENTERTAINMENT WITH SEVERAL BANDS AND MANY WELL KNOWN SINGERS. THE WHOLE DAY WAS ONE GREAT BIG SHOW.

THERE WERE HUNDREDS OF PEOPLE TO BE SERVED WITH FOOD AND DRINK AND WE, ALONG WITH SEVERAL OTHER CATERING OUTFITS DID THE SERVING.

I SAW BOB HOPE, BUT NEVER GOT VERY CLOSE TO HIM.

THE CATERING JOB THAT I REMEMBERED THE MOST AND FOR GOOD REASON WAS HELD AT A RADIO STATION IN CHICAGO. IT WAS IN A THEATER LIKE ROOM, WITH A STAGE AND SEATING SO THAT PEOPLE COULD WATCH THE RADIO SHOW AS IT WAS BEING BROADCASTED.

IT WAS A BIRTHDAY PARTY AND WAS HELD UP ON THE STAGE. WE SET UP ENOUGH FOLDING CHAIRS AND TABLES

TO ACCOMMODATE SIXTY PEOPLE. WE BROUGHT ALONG A PORTABLE BAR AND A JUKE-BOX. THERE WAS A GOOD SIZE EMPTY ROOM NEXT TO THE STAGE, ITS WALLS WERE LINED WITH SHELVES. WE FIGURED THAT THE ROOM WAS USED AS A PROP ROOM DURING A BROADCAST, IT WAS HANDY AND WE USED IT AS A STOREROOM FOR OUR SUPPLIES AND EQUIPMENT.

WE BROUGHT WITH US TWO PORTABLE REFRIGERATORS ON WHEELS. THEY WERE LARGE ENOUGH TO HOLD THE BIRTHDAY CAKE AND THE PERISHABLE FOOD. WE ALSO BROUGHT SOME HOT-PLATES, THE SOUP AND SOME OF THE FOOD WOULD BE SERVED HOT.

WE ALWAYS DOUBLE CHECKED, BEFORE WE LEFT OUR RESTAURANT, THAT WE HAD THE RIGHT EQUIPMENT AND MORE THAN ENOUGH FOOD AND DRINKS FOR THE EVENT WE WERE WORKING. THAT WAS MY JOB.

WE ARRIVED AT THE RADIO STATION TWO HOURS EARLY SO THAT WE HAD PLENTY OF TIME TO GET SET UP BEFORE THE GUESTS BEGAN TO ARRIVE. THE FIRST HALF HOUR OF THE PARTY WENT SMOOTHLY, THE PEOPLE WERE HAVING DRINKS AND TALKING IN SMALL GROUPS. THEN THERE WAS A SUDDEN COMMOTION, EVERYONE WAS STANDING AND APPLAUDING. THE GUEST OF HONOR HAD ARRIVED ALONG WITH HER TWO SISTERS. SHE WAS PATTIE ANDREW OF THE ANDREW SISTERS SINGING GROUP. PATTIE WAS THE BLOND, LEAD SINGER THAT ALWAYS STOOD IN BETWEEN HER TWO

Ronald M. Gifford

DARK HAIRED SISTERS WHEN THEY SANG. THERE WERE THE TOP FEMALE SINGING GROUP DURING THE WORLD WAR TWO ERA.

THEY DIDN'T SAY ANYTHING, THEY WAVED AND WENT STRAIGHT TO THE MICROPHONE AND SANG SEVERAL OF THEIR BIG HITS SONGS. WHEN THEY HAD FINISHED SINGING THEY STARTED WALKING, WITH BIG SMILES ON THEIR FACES AMONG THE TABLES OF PEOPLE WHERE EVERYONE WAS APPLAUDING AND WAITING TO GREET THEM.

I WAS BENT OVER FILLING THE WATER GLASSES AT THE HEAD TABLE WHEN I HEARD PATTIE ANDREW SAY IN A LOUD VOICE, I KNOW WHAT I WANT FOR MY BIRTHDAY.

I STRAIGHTENED UP AND HALF TURNED AROUND AND COULD SEE THAT SHE WAS WALKING IN MY DIRECTION. SHE STOPPED IN FRONT OF ME AND PUT HER HANDS ON MY SHOULDERS. THEN LOOKED AROUND AT THE GUESTS AND SAID, THIS IS WHAT I WANT FOR MY BIRTHDAY.

THE CROWD WAS ALREADY LAUGHING AND CLAPPING THEIR HANDS AND WHEN SHE THREW HER ARMS AROUND ME AND KISSED ME ON THE CHEEK, THEY REALLY ROARED. THEY PROBABLY THOUGHT THAT THIS WAS PRE-ARRANGED AND STAGED FOR THEM.

IT TOOK ME SO MUCH BY SURPRISE THAT I KNOW THAT I HAD A DUMB LOOK ON MY FACE. WHEN SHE TOOK A

STEP BACK AND LOOKED INTO MY FACE AND EYES, HER HAPPY SMILE TURNED SERIOUS AND WORRIED. THEN INTO A SMILE AGAIN. SHE HUGGED ME AND WHISPERED INTO MY EAR, I'M SORRY, I DIDN'T......

AT THAT MOMENT I REMEMBERED PETES WORDS. 'IT ISN'T PERSONAL. WE'RE REAL AND DOING A JOB'. I WHISPERED BACK TO HER, IT'S OK AND KISSED HER ON THE CHEEK.

I STOOD THERE LIKE A WOODEN POST AND WATCHED HER WALK TO HER SEAT AND SIT DOWN. IT MUST HAVE BEEN AN HILARIOUS SIGHT, ME IN MY WHITE WAITERS JACKET, WHITE SHIRT AND BLACK BOW TIE WITH BLOND HAIR AND I'M SURE BEET-RED FACE. AFTER A FEW MOMENTS I WENT BACK TO FILLING WATER GLASSES. I GOT SOME GOOD NATURED REMARKS FROM THE MEN AND SOME KINDLY SMILES FROM THE LADIES. I TRIED TO SMILE THROUGH IT ALL BUT I DIDN'T KNOW IF MY SMILE WAS WORKING VERY WELL AT THE TIME.

THE DINNER WENT WELL. EVERYONE SEEMED TO BE SATISFIED WITH THE FOOD AND THE SERVICE. IT WAS A NICE POLITE CROWD.

THE BIRTHDAY CAKE WAS ALREADY LIT WHEN WE BROUGHT IT IN. PATTY, WITH THE HELP OF HER SISTERS BLEW OUT THE CANDLES AND EVERYONE, INCLUDING US WAITERS SANG HAPPY BIRTHDAY TO PATTIE. THERE WAS SOME ENTERTAINMENT, A MALE SINGER, SOME

DANCERS AND A COMIC. THEN A PORTLY, OLDER MAN REPRESENTING THE BROADCASTING COMPANY STEPPED TO THE MIKE AND SAID THAT IT WAS A GREAT HONOR TO HAVE BEEN INVITED TO THE PARTY AND HE WISHED PATTIE AND HER SISTERS MANY MORE YEARS OF THEIR REAL SUCCESS. IN THE MEANTIME WE HAD CLEARED THE TABLES, PLUGGED IN THE JUKE-BOX AND TURNED IT ON. WE HAD SELECTED SOME GOOD DANCE MUSIC RECORDS AND THE GUESTS STARTED DANCING. SOME FOLKS WERE AT THE BAR, WHILE OTHERS WERE SITTING AT TABLES TALKING AND LAUGHING AND APPARENTLY HAVING A GOOD TIME.

THE ANDREW SISTERS WENT FROM GROUP TO GROUP MINGLING AND SIGNING AUTOGRAPSH, IT WAS A NICE ORDERLY AFFAIR. PERFECT FOR US; IT CAME OFF JUST AS WE HAD PLANNED AND HOPED EVERY PARTY WOULD BE. THE PARTY BROKE UP AT ABOUT ONE A.M. AND WE WERE ABOUT DONE WITH THIS JOB. ALL WE HAD LEFT TO DO WAS TO FOLD UP THE CHAIRS AND TABLES AND LOAD THEM INTO THE TRUCK, TURN OUT THE LIGHTS AND LOCK THE DOOR.

I WAS BENT OVER FOLDING AND STACKING CHAIRS IN A PILE WHEN I FELT A TAP ON MY SHOULDER. I STRAIGHTENED UP AND TURNED AND WAS STANDING FACE TO FACE WITH PATTIE ANDREW.

I WAS CALM AND ALERT THIS TIME AND SAID HAPPY BIRTHDAY.

SHE GAVE A SMALL LAUGH AND SAID, YOU'RE TOO LATE, IT'S THE NEXT DAY NOW.

WE BOTH SMILED BRAODLY AND SHE WENT ON. I DIDN'T MEAN TO EMBARRESS YOU. IT WAS JUST A SPUR OF THE MOMENT QUICK JOKE, MEANT TO LOOSEN UP THE CROWD.

I SAID, I UNDERSTAND. I DO A LOT OF THESE PARTIES AND I'VE SEEN A LOT OF GOOFY THINGS HAPPEN, BUT THIS WAS THE FIRST TIME THAT I'VE BEEN INVOLVED. AS SOON AS I CAME OUT OF MY COMA I REALIZED THAT IT WASN'T PERSONAL, IT WAS YOUR WAY OF GREETING YOUR GUESTS.

SHE SAID, THEN YOUR NOT MAD OR HATE ME?

HECK NO I SAID, IT WAS A GOOD LEARNING EXPERIENCE FOR ME. IT HAPPENED SO FAST THAT I DIDN'T KNOW HOW TO REACT.

SHE SAID WELL GREAT, YOU'RE A GOOD SPORT AND SHE STUCK OUT HER HAND.

I TOOK IT AND WE SHOOK HANDS.

SHE SAID IT WAS NICE MEETING YOU. I ANSWERED, LIKE WISE, AND SHE TURNED AND WALKED OVER TO WHERE HER SISTERS AND THEIR DRIVER WERE STANDING. THEY ALL WAVED AND WERE GONE.

SHE HAD PUT SOMETHING IN MY HAND WHEN WE SHOOK. I LOOKED DOWN AND OPENED MY FINGERS AND COULD SEE THAT IT WAS FOLDED MONEY. I SHOVED IT INTO MY POCKET AND RESUMED FOLDING CHAIRS. WHEN WE GOT BACK TO THE RESTAURANT PARKING LOT IN PETES CAR HE SAID, I'M SORRY THAT YOU GOT EMBARRASSED TONIGHT BUT YOU HANDLED IT PRETTY GOOD.

I SAID, IT'S OK, I CAN LIVE WITH IT, AND BESIDES SHE APOLOGIZED WHEN IT HAPPENED AND AGAIN AS SHE WAS LEAVING.

PETE LOOKED AT ME IN AMAZEMENT AND SAID, YOU KNOW WHAT, I'VE HAD BAD THOUGHTS ABOUT HER ALL EVENING. I GUESS MAYBE THE LADY HAS GOT SOME CLASS AFTER ALL.

I AGREED THAT INDEED SHE DID HAVE. GOT OUT OF HIS CAR AND SAID GOODNIGHT PETE. SEE YOU MONDAY.

PETE PULLED AWAY AND I WALKED OVER TO THE BACK PORCH OF THE RESTAURANT. UNDER THE LIGHT THAT WAS OVER THE DOOR I PULLED THE MONEY THAT PATTIE HAD GIVEN ME OUT OF MY POCKET. IT WAS FOLDED UP REAL SMALL AND WHEN I UNFOLDED IT I WAS AMAZED. IT WAS A ONE HUNDRED DOLLAR BILL. I HAD SEEN THEM BEFORE BUT THIS WAS THE FIRST ONE I HAD EVER HELD IN MY HAND. I TURNED IT OVER AND LOOKED DOWN AT

IT AND GUESSED THAT IT WAS MY REWARD FOR BEING SUCH A DUMB CLUCK.

I NEVER DID TELL ANYONE THE STORY ABOUT THE HUNDRED DOLLAR BILL NOT EVEN PETE......

A STRANGE UNKNOWN WORLD

ONE VERY DARK EARLY SPRING DAY AS I WAS DRIVING
HOME FROM WORK, AT TWO A.M. IN THE MORNING, I
HAD THE ODD FEELING THAT I WAS NO LONGER IN OR
OF THE SAME WORLD THAT I HAD BEEN A PART OF A FEW
HOURS BEFORE.

STREETS AND OTHER LANDMARKS THAT I KNEW WELL,
WERE NO LONGER FAMILIAR TO ME. TREE BRANCHES
AND OTHER DEBRIS WERE SHREWN EVERYWHERE,
CARELESSLY TOSSED AROUND BY THE UNRULLY
HURRICANE LIKE WINDS OF THE LAST FEW HOURS OF
A LONG NIGHT. NOW ALL THAT REMAINED OF THE
NATURES ELEMENTS WAS A LIGHT RAIN ACCOMPANIED
BY A GENTLE BREEZE.

THERE WERE NONE OF THE USUAL CITY NOISES TO BE
HEARD. THE ONLY LIGHTS TO BE SEEN WERE ON THE
SLOW MOVING CARS AND TRUCKS THAT CRAWLED THE
CLUTTERED STREETS. OUR USUALLY TENSION FILLED
WORLD HAD TAKEN ON A PEACEFUL CALMNESS THAT
WAS MOVING IN SLOW MOTION AND WAS DREAMLIKE.

I WAS QUITE PROUD OF THE WAY THAT THE OTHER HEADLIGHTS WERE BEHAVING. THERE WAS NO HUSTLE OR BUSTLE, NO FIGHTING TO BE FIRST. THE CARS SEEMED TO BE BANDING TOGETHER IN SMALL CROUPS OF THREES AND FOURS, AS IF SEEKING COMPANIONSHIP.

ALTHOUGH ALL OF THE STOP LIGHTS AT THE INTERSECTIONS WERE OUT AND NOT WORKING, THE HEADLIGHTS ALL WERE STOPPING AND PAUSING AT THEM, BEFORE CONTINUING ON THEIR WAY. IT SEEMED AS THOUGH TIME WAS OF NO IMPORTANCE TO ANYONE.

THE NEXT DAY DRIVING TO WORK IT WAS OBVIOUS TO ME THAT THINGS WERE ONCE AGAIN BACK TO THEIR NORMALLY CONFUSED STATE. CARS WERE JACK-RABBITING AWAY FROM STOP SIGNS, AND HORNS WERE TOOT-TOOTING AND BEEP-BEEPING ANGRILY AT ONE ANOTHER.

SPORTS MODELS, CONVENTIONALS AND PICK-UP TRUCKS WERE FRANTICALLY RACING EACH OTHER FOR SMALL, MOMENTARILY VACANT PIECES OF PAVEMENT, SO THAT THEY COULD ARRIVE AT THEIR DESTINATIONS A FEW HECTIC MINUTES EARLIER THEN SAFETY PERMITS.

IS THE QUIET, PEACEFUL, COURTEOUS, SERENE FANTASY THAT I HAD WITNESSED THE DAY BEFORE A POSSIBILITY IN THE FUTURE, OR ARE WE MORTALS DOOMED TO PLAY FOREVER THE GAME THAT WE HAVE DEVISED FOR OURSELVES CALLED, "THE RAT RACE"......

BASEBALL THE GAME THE FAN-ATIC

IT WAS DADS FAULT. HE'S THE ONLY ONE THAT I CAN THINK OF TO TAKE MY FRUSTRATIONS OUT ON. I'VE GOT TO BLAME SOMEONE. THIS WHOLE THING STARTED BACK IN THE TWENTIES IN A SMALL FARMING TOWN IN IOWA, IN THE LAND OF TALL CORN.

WE WERE A FAMILY OF FOUR, MOM, DAD, SIS AND ME. DAD WORKED HARD TRYING TO SCRATCH OUT A LIVING FOR HIS FAMILY. MOM DID HER PART. THINGS WEREN'T WORKING OUT TOO WELL FOR THE YOUNG PEOPLE IN THE POST WAR DAYS OF WORLD WAR ONE.

DAD HAD SERVED WITH BLACK JACK PERSHINGS ARMY DURING THE WAR IN EUROPE AND HAD SURVIVED THAT AS WELL AS THE GREAT FLU EPIDEMIC. THE SMALL TOWN BOY HAD SEEN A CHUNK OF THE WORLD AND SOME OF THE BIG CITIES IN AMERICA. ALL THESE THINGS MAY HAVE CHANGED HIS PROSPECTIVE, HIS WAY OF THINKING.

DAD WORKED FOR A RAILROAD PART TIME AS A SECTION HAND AND ALSO FILLED IN AT THE CAFÉ IN TOWN AS A

SHORT ORDER COOK. NEITHER JOB WAS PERMENT OR STEADY.

WE LIVED IN THE THREE ROOM HOUSE WHERE I WAS BORN, IT WAS ABOUT AS BIG AS A TWO CAR GARAGE, WE ATE MOSTLY FROM THE LARGE GARDEN MOM KEPT OUT IN BACK AND A SMALL FLOCK OF CHICKENS. SOMETIMES GRANDMA BROUGHT OVER SOME SAMPLES. IT COULD HAVE BEEN WORST.

BEING A YOUNG MAN WITH ENERGY AND AMBITIONS, DAD THOUGHT THAT CHICAGO MIGHT BE THE ANSWER TO OUR FUTURE. HE DECIDED TO GO TO CHICAGO, THE BIG CITY AND TRY TO FIND A STEADY JOB. IF HE COULDN'T FIND ANYTHING WORTHWHILE, HE'D COME BACK AND DO AS GOOD AS HE COULD. WE MOVED IN WITH GRANDMOTHER.

DAD FOUND A FULL TIME JOB ON A RAILROAD AS A TRAINMAN AND WE JOINED HIM IN A FEW WEEKS. RIGHT THEN AND THERE, AT THE AGE OF TEN MONTHS, MY PROBLEM WAS TO START, ALTHOUGH I WASN'T TO LEARN ABOUT IT FOR SOME YEARS.

WE MOVED INTO A FURNISHED APPARTMENT ON THE SOUTHWEST SIDE OF CHICAGO, WEST OF MIDWAY AIRPORT. THE AIRPORT WAS KNOWN AS THE MUNICIPAL AIRPORT BACK THEN. OUR COMMUNITY WAS SITUATED ON THE WESTERN EDGE OF THE CITY AND WAS CALLED CLEARING. WE HAD RADIO, BUT OF COURSE NOT

TELEVISION YET. THERE WAS PLENTY TO DO WITHOUT EITHER.

CLEARING WAS A GREAT PLACE TO GROW UP IN. I HAD A NODDING AQUAINTANCE WITH ABOUT HALF THE PEOPLE IN THE AREA, YOUNG AND OLD. IT WAS LIKE LIVING IN A SMALL TOWN.

WE PLAYED GAMES WITH THE NEIGHBORHOOD KIDS UNTIL THE STREET LIGHTS WENT ON, THAT WAS THE SIGNAL THAT IT WAS SUPPER TIME AND EVERYBODY WENT HOME.

WE LISTENED TO THE LONE RANGER, JACK ARMSTRONG AND LITTLE ORPHAN ANNIE ON THE RADIO WHILE EATING SUPPER. WITH THE QUARTER ALLOWANCE THAT I GOT EVERY SATURDAY I COULD GO TO A DOUBLE-FEATURE MOVIE, BUY SOME PENNY CANDY AND STILL HAVE MONEY JINGLING IN MY POCKET. LIFE WAS GREAT.

JUST ABOUT EVERYBODY WERE FRIENDS OR FRIENDLY. I HAD SCHOOL FRIENDS, NEIGHBORHOOD FRIENDS, SUNDAY SCHOOL FRIENDS AND SPORTS GAMES FRIENDS. I EVEN HAD AN AIRPLANE FRIEND NAMED EARL. WE'D WALK OVER TO THE AIRPORT AND WATCH THE AIRPLANES COME AND GO, TAKE OFF AND LAND. SOMETIMES WE'D WATCH FOR HOURS. EARL JOINED THE ARMY AIR FORCE DURING WORLD WAR TWO, AND LATER BECAME A COMMERICAL AIRLINE PILOT. I GUESS HE WAS MORE SERIOUS ABOUT AIRPLANES THAN I WAS.

MY WORST NIGHTMARE CAME IN THE SUMMER OF 1938.

DAD WORKED THE NIGHT SHIFT AND THAT MORNING HE MUST HAVE COME RIGHT HOME, CLEANED UP AND ATE BREAKFAST BECAUSE IT WAS STILL EARLY WHEN HE WOKE ME. HE SHOOK ME AND SAID, COME ON BUD, GET UP AND GET DRESSED AND HAVE SOME BREAKFAST WE'RE GOING OUT TO A BALL GAME.

I SAT UP IN BED AND JUST LOOKED AT HIM. THERE WERE TWO GOOD BASEBALL TEAMS IN OUR AREA AND WE WATCHED THEM WHENEVER THEY WERE PLAYING HERE, BUT IT WAS USUALLY ON THE WEEKEND AND THIS WAS THE MIDDLE OF THE WEEK.

DAD MUST HAVE READ MY MIND BECAUSE HE SAID, WE'RE GOING OUT TO COMISKEY PARK TO WATCH THE WHITE SOX AND PHILADELPHIA PLAY. HE WAS REAL EXCITED AND WANTED ME TO HURRY. HE WENT ON, COMISKEY PARK IS WAY OVER, THE OTHER SIDE OF THE CHICAGO STOCKYARDS AND WE'VE GOT A LONG STREETCAR RIDE, SO SHAKE IT UP. DAD HAD PICKED THE WHITE SOX AS HIS TEAM AND ALTHOUGH HE HADN'T SEEN A GAME YET, HE FOLLOWED THEM EVERY DAY IN THE NEWSPAPERS.

IT WAS A LONG WAY OVER TO THE PARK BUT WE WERE GOING TO SEE A BIG LEAGUE GAME SO IT'D BE WORTH IT.

WE GOT THERE IN PLENTY OF TIME TO WATCH BATTING AND INFIELD PRACTICE. DAD STUDIED HIS SCORECARD

FOR A WHILE AND THEN LOOKED OUT AT THE FIELD. FINALLY HE SAID TO ME, THERE HE IS, THAT'S WHO I WANTED US TO SEE. HE WAS POINTING AT A STOUT OLDER MAN IN A BASEBALL UNIFORM WHO WAS STANDING ALONE IN FRONT OF THE VISITERS DUGOUT, LOOKING OUT AT THE INFIELD. DAD WENT ON, THAT'S TY COBB. HE'S ONE OF THE GREATEST BALLPLAYERS OF ALL TIME. LOOKING AT HIM, I COULDN'T SEE HIS GREATNESS, IT DIDN'T SHOW. DAD WENT ON, TY COBB HOLDS MANY BASEBALL RECORDS.

I WASN'T IMPRESSED.

IN LATER YEARS, WHEN I LEARNED AND UNDERSTOOD ABOUT THE HISTORY OF BASEBALL, I WAS GLAD THAT DAD HAD TAKEN ME TO SEE THE GREAT TY COBB.

MR. COBB DIDN'T HAVE ANYTHING TO DO WITH MY PROBLEM, BUT BEING IN BASEBALL, HE WAS A PART OF IT.

IT ALL STARTED THAT DAY IN COMISKEY PARK. SOMETHING HAPPENED TO DAD THAT DAY AT OUR FIRST BIG LEAGUE GAME.

DAD WAS BIT, BIG TIME BY THE BASEBALL BUG. I GUESS YOU COULD SAY THAT HE HAD BECOME ADDICTED ON THE SPOT.

MAYBE IT'S IN THE GENES OR INHERITED BECAUSE I BECAME AN ADDICT TOO THAT DAY, I WAS BITTEN BY THE SAME BUG.

WE DIDN'T GO OUT TO WRIGLEY FIELD MUCH; WE ONLY WENT TO THE CUBS BALL PARK WHEN THERE WAS A SPECIAL PLAYER OR TEAM THAT DAD WANTED TO SEE.

THE WHITE SOX WERE OUR BALL TEAM, SO WE WENT OUT TO COMISKEY PARK WHENEVER WE COULD, WHICH WAS HUNDREDS OF TIMES THROUGH THE YEARS.

I WAS HOOKED, WE BOTH WERE, AND BASEBALL WAS IN OUR BLOOD. IF YOU'VE EVER BEEN ADDICTED TO ANYTHING, YOU KNOW HOW IT IS, THE MORE YOU GET, THE MORE YOU WANT. NO MATTER HOW BAD THINGS MIGHT BE.

WE WENT OUT TO WATCH THE WHITE SOX THROUGH THE YEARS. THE PLAYERS ON THE TEAM DIDN'T CHANGE AS MUCH FROM YEAR TO YEAR AS THEY DO NOW AND THE RESULTS DIDN'T CHANGE MUCH EITHER.

THE SOX LOST MORE GAMES THEN THEY WON MOST YEARS. THERE WERE EIGHT TEAMS IN EACH LEAGUE THEN AND TWO DIVISIONS IN EACH. THE SOX USUALLY ENDED UP IN THE SECOND DIVISION OF THE AMERICAN LEAGUE ALONG WITH THE ST. LOUIS BROWNS AND THE WASHINGTON SENATORS. AT FIRST IT DIDN'T MATTER WHERE THE SOX ENDED UP BUT AFTER A FEW YEARS IT

DID START TO MATTER. IT REALLY HURT DEEP DOWN INSIDE ME, LIKE A BIG LEAD BALL LAYING IN MY STOMACH. I GOT TO FEELING LIKE I WAS A FAILURE. THE LOSSES WERE DISRUPTING OTHER PARTS OF MY LIFE. ALL WINTER WE'D TRY TO CONVINCE OURSELVES THAT THE TEAM WOULD BE BETTER IN THE COMING SEASON, BUT IT SELDOM WAS.

LIFE IN GENERAL REMAINED GOOD UNTIL 1929, THEN THE DEPRESSION HIT. WE WERE IN THE SAME BOAT WITH JUST ABOUT EVERYONE ELSE THAT WE KNEW. SOME BOATS HAD MORE HOLES IN THEM OTHERS. IT WAS A STRUGGLE FOR JUST ABOUT EVERYBODY. DAD WAS ONE OF THE FORTUNATE ONES. HE NEVER GOT LAID OFF, BUT HE WAS CUT DOWN TO TWO OR THREE DAYS A WEEK. MOM FOUND A JOB IN A RADIO FACTORY THAT PAID HER SEVEN DOLLARS A WEEK FOR FORTY HOURS OF WORK. SEVEN DOLLARS DOESN'T SOUND LIKE MUCH NOW, BUT YOU COULD FEED A FAMILY OF FOUR ON GOOD STAPLE FOOD FOR FIVE OR SIX DOLLARS A WEEK THEN. NOBODY MADE ENOUGH MONEY TO PAY TAXES. MOM WAS WORKING DAYS AND DAD WORKED NIGHTS WHEN HE COULD WORK, SO MY SISTER AND I WERE PART TIME LATCH-KEY KID FOR SEVERAL YEARS. MOM WOULD WAKE SIS AND I WHEN SHE WAS LEAVING FOR WORK IN THE MORNING AND DAD WOULD ALREADY BE IN BED SLEEPING, SO SIS AND I WOULD MAKE OUR OWN BREAKFASTS. I LEARNED TO FRY EGGS WHEN I WAS SIX. EGGS WERE CHEAP. SOMETIMES WE HAD THEM FRIED FOR BREAKFAST, EGG SANDICHES FOR LUNCH AND HAD THEM SCRAMBLED WITH CHOPPED HOT-DOGS FOR

SUPPER. MOM KNEW HOW TO FIX EGGS DOZENS OF WAYS. HAMBURGER WAS ALSO VERY CHEAP SO WE ATE A LOT OF HAMBURGER. MOMS SPAGHETTE AND HAMBURGER WAS OUT OF THIS WORLD, I'VE NEVER BEEN ABLE TO DUPLICATE IT. IN 1933 THERE WAS A WORLDS FAIR HELD IN CHICAGO AND THEY CALLED IT, 'A CENTURY OF PROGRESS', PRETTY SILLY TITLE FOR A COUNTRY THAT WAS IN THE MIDDLE OF ONE OF ITS WORST DEPRESSIONS EVER. TO US KIDS IT WAS A WONDERLAND, AN OASIS IN THE MIDST OF A GLOOMY TIME.

THE MOST IMPORTANT THING TO HAPPEN IN 1933, AS FAR AS I WAS CONCERNED WAS THE VERY FIRST MAJOR LEAGUE ALL-STAR BASEBALL GAME AND IT WAS BEING PLAYED IN CHICAGO, IN COMISKEY PARK, HOME OF OUR OWN WHITE SOX. IT WAS ABOUT ALL THAT THE BOYS IN MY NEIGHBORHOOD COULD TALK ABOUT FOR DAYS, OF COURSE NONE OF US COULD EVEN DREAM OF GOING TO IT, BUT YOU COULD BET THAT WE'D ALL BE GLUED TO OUR RADIOS FOR EVERY PLAY.

WE WERE ABOUT HALFWAY THROUGH EATING SUPPER ON THE NIGHT BEFORE THE BIG GAME WHEN DAD SAID TO NO ONE IN PARTICULAR, GUESS WHERE I'M GOING TOMORROW? NO ONE ANSWERED. I NOTICED THAT MOM HAD A HINT OF A SMILE ON HER FACE, LIKE SHE KNEW BUT WASN'T GOING TO TELL. DAD TOOK AN ENVELOPE FROM HIS SHIRT POCKET AND HELD IT UP AND THEN SAID, THERE'S A TICKET TO THE ALL-STAR GAME IN THE ENVELOPE AND I'M GOING TO THE GAME TOMORROW.

SIS AND I BOTH GAVE DAD A LOOK THAT SAID WE DIDN'T BELIEVE HIM. DAD REACHED ACROSS THE TABLE AND DROPPED THE ENVELOPE IN FRONT OF ME AND SAID, HAVE A LOOK FOR YOURSELF.

I DIDN'T KNOW IF DAD WAS PULLING ONE OF HIS TRICKS OR NOT BUT I LOOKED INSIDE THE ENVELOPE ANYWAY. THERE WERE TWO TICKETS AND THEY WERE FOR THE ALL-STAR GAME. I LOOKED UP AND HELD THE TWO TICKETS IN MY FINGERS AND ALL THREE OF THEM WERE BEAMING WITH WIDE SMILES ON THEIR FACES.

DAD LOOKED FROM THE TICKETS UP TO MY FACE AND SAID, WELL BUD, IF THERE ARE TWO TICKETS THERE; YOU'RE GOING TO HAVE TO GO WITH ME.

THEY ALL LAUGHED, THE THREE OF THEM HAD KNOWN THE SURPRISE. IT WAS THE BEST JOKE ANYONE EVER PULLED ON ME. I WAS STUNNED, IN A DAZE. NEVER IN MY WILDEST DREAMS DID I THINK THAT I WOULD BE GOING TO THE GAME.

I DIDN'T SLEEP MUCH THAT NIGHT, IT WAS LIKE CHRISTMAS EVE, ONLY MORE SO. EXCITEMENT AND ANTICIPATION FILLED MY HEAD.

DAD NEVER DID TELL ME WHERE AND HOW HE GOT THE TICKETS. I SUSPECT HE PAID A PRETTY PENNY FOR THEM.

THE BALL PARK WAS FILLING UP FAST BY THE TIME WE WERE ABLE TO GET IN. OUR SEATS WERE IN THE UPPER DECK IN RIGHT FIELD, JUST INSIDE THE FOUL LINE.

DURING BATTING PRACTICE LOU GEHRIG OF THE NEW YORK YANKEES HIT A BALL RIGHT OVER MY HEAD. I DIDN'T GET THE BALL BUT IT WAS A LINE DRIVE AND I CAN STILL HEAR IT WHISTLING AS IT FLEW A FEW FEET OVER MY HEAD.

THE BALL PARK WAS PACKED, BUT THE PEOPLE WERE DIFFERENT THAN THE FANS I WAS USE TO. THESE PEOPLE WERE LAUGHING AND TALKING LOUD AND STIRRING AROUND, IT WAS REALLY NOISY. THE REGULAR FANS I KNEW, FOCUSED ON THE GAME, ON EVERY PITCH, EVERY PLAY. THEY ONLY CHEERED WHEN THE HOME TEAM HAD A RALLY GOING OR THERE WAS AN OUTSTANDING PLAY MADE. I DIDN'T THINK THAT THE PEOPLE THAT WERE THERE THAT DAY WERE REAL BASEBALL FANS, I THINK THEY WERE THERE JUST FOR THE EVENT.

ANYWAY IT WAS TERRIFIC JUST BEING THERE THAT DAY AND SEEING MOST OF THE BEST BASEBALL PLAYERS IN THE WORLD ALL IN ONE PLACE. I HAD SEEN MOST OF THE AMERICAN LEAGUE PLAYERS BUT NOT MANY OF THE NATIONAL LEAGUERS.

IF YOU'VE EVER LIVED IN A CITY WITH TWO MAJOR LEAGUE TEAMS, YOU KNOW THAT YOU CAN'T BE TRULY LOYAL TO BOTH TEAMS. YOU PICK OUT ONE OF THE

TEAMS AS YOUR TEAM AND PRETTY MUCH IGNORE THE OTHER TEAM. IT CAN LEAD TO SOME GOOD NATURED KIDDING AMONG FRIENDS, COMPARING PLAYERS AT DIFFERENT POSITIONS ON BOTH TEAMS. DAD PICKED THE WHITE SOX AS OUR TEAM SO WE WERE AMERICAN LEAGUERS AND DIDN'T KNOW MUCH ABOUT THE PLAYAERS IN THE NATIONAL LEAGUE.

IT WAS A PRETTY GOOD GAME, THE AMERICAN LEAGUE WON FOUR TO TWO AND IT LOOKED LIKE MOST PEOPLE WENT AWAY HAPPY. I HOPED THEY WOULD CONTINUE HAVING THE GAMES, IT WAS A GOOD IDEA. THE GAME WAS THE BRAIN CHILD OF ARCH WARD, A SPORTS WRITER FOR THE CHICAGO TRIBUNE. I THINK HE WAS ALSO IN THE PLANNING OF THE COLLEGE ALL-STAR FOOTBALL GAME, THE SILVER SKATES AND THE GOLDEN GLOVES BOXING TOURNAMENTS. I DON'T KNOW THAT MR. WARD HAS GOTTEN PROPER CREDIT FOR THESE EVENTS. I GUESS MOST PEOPLE DON'T KNOW OR CARE HOW THEY ALL GOT STARTED.

WE SAT IN OUR SEATS, PERCHED HIGH UP IN THE FAR CORNER OF RIGHT FIELD FOR QUITE A WHILE. DAD WANTED TO WAIT UNTIL THE TRAFFIC HAD THINNED OUT SOME AND SAT LOOKING AT HIS SCORECARD.

I LOOKED OUT AT THE ACRES OF GRASS, THE INFIELD, THE DUGOUTS AND THE GRANSTANDS AND DREAMED A LITTLE BOYS DREAM. MAYBE IF SOMEDAY I GOT GOOD ENOUGH, I COULD PLAY ON THAT FIELD. THE WHITE SOX

FINALLY WON THE PENNANT IN 1959. IT WAS THE FIRST TIME THEY HAD DONE IT IN MY LIFE AND I COULDN'T GET TICKETS. I CYNICALLY SUSPECTED THAT THE SAME POPLE ATTENDED THE GAMES THAT WERE AT THE FIRST ALL-STAR GAME IN 1933, BEING SEEN AND MAKING NOISE AND JUST HAVING FUN. THE SOX LOST TO THE L.A. DODGERS IN SIX GAMES AND THE WHOLE THING TOOK MOST OF THE WIND OUT OF THE SAILS.

I LEFT CHICAGO YEARS LATER AND MOVED TO NEW MEXICO. I DON'T LOOK FOR THE BOX SCORES IN THE PAPER MUCH, I DO WATCH A GAME NOW AND THEN ON TELEVISION. I'VE BEEN WITHDRAWAL FOR YEARS. ADDICTS ARE NEVER REALLY CURED. I'M STILL A SOX FAN. THE WAY I LOOK AT IT, THERE'S ONLY TWO THINGS A BROKEN DOWN HARDCORE BASEBALL NUT CAN DO TO GET IT OUT OF HIS SYSTEM. HE CAN MOVE TO A FOREIGN COUNTRY WHERE THERE'S NO ENGLISH SPOKEN AND THERE'S NO CONTACT WITH THE OUTSIDE WORLD OR HE CAN TAKE A JUMP OFF OF A HIGH PIER. IT'S NOT MUCH OF A CHOICE EITHER WAY. IF DAD WERE HERE TODAY, I'D ASK HIM JUST ONE QUESTION. WHY DIDN'T HE GO TO NEW YORK AND LOOK FOR WORK? WE COULD HAVE BEEN YANKEE FANS CHEERING FOR BABE RUTH, LOU GEHRIG, MICKEY MANTLE AND ALL THE REST OF THE GREAT YANKEE PLAYERS, WE COULD HAVE BEEN WINNERS. I COULD NOW BE READING THE SPORT PAGES AND STUDYING THE SOX SCORES INSTEAD OF READING THE FUNNY PAPERS......

MY QUIET WORLD

FIVE O'CLOCK IN THE MORNING UNDER SOME CIRCUMSTANCES IS CONSIDERED AN UNHOLY HOUR, BUT IF YOU HAPPEN TO BE A LOVER OF NATURE OR A FISHERMAN, IT MIGHT BE YOUR MOST FAVORITE TIME OF THE DAY. ESPECIALLY IF YOU'RE ON A SMALL, CALM LAKE IN NORTHERN MINNESOTA.

THIS PARTICULAR MORNING, AS I WAS PREPARING FOR MY DAILY OUTING, MY THOUGHTS WERE NOT EXACTLY ON THE HAPPY SIDE. I THOUGHT, IT WON'T BE MORE THEN AN HOUR BEFORE HE WILL BE TIRED OR HUNGRY OR HAVE A CRAMP IN HIS LEG OR SOME OTHER SUCH THING AND WE'LL HAVE TO COME IN TO SHORE. AN ABRUPT ENDING TO A FINE BEAUTIFUL MORNING. THERE WAS NO USE IN COMPLAINING NOW THAT I HAD GIVEN IN TO THE PLEADINGS OF MY SEVEN YEAR OLD SON MARK, I WOULD MAKE THE MOST OF IT AND TAKE HIM OUT THIS ONCE, INTO MY QUIET WORLD.

I HAVE NO OBJECTIONS TO TAKING ANY AND EVERYBODY FISHING LATER IN THE DAY. I BAIT ALL HOOKS, NET AND STRING THE FISH, ACT AS GUIDE, TEND THE ANCHOR

AND BE HAPPY FOR THE COMPANY, BUT THE QUIET, COOL EARLY MORNINGS HAD BECOME SOMETHING SPECIAL TO ME. IT WAS MORE OF A RELAXING TIME THAN AN ACTIVE FISHING TRIP. I WOULD JUST LAZE ALONG AND ENJOY THE STILLNESS AND SERENITY OF PRE-DAWN. NOT REALLY WANTING TO THINK OR DO ANYTHING THAT WOULD CONNECT ME TO THE OUTSIDE WORLD. THESE WERE I THINK, THE MOST PEACEFUL TIMES THAT I HAVE EVER KNOWN. A LITTLE LATER, AS I SAT THERE ENTRANCED IN WONDER, THE WORLD AGAIN CAME TO LIFE AROUND ME WITH THE SCURRING OF THE LITTLE FOREST ANIMALS AND THE CHATTERING AND MORNING SONGS OF THE LARGE VARIETY OF BIRDS.

I THINK THAT IT MUST HAVE BEEN A SELFISH JEALOUSY THAT MADE ME UNWILLING TO SHARE THESE SPECIAL MORNING WITH ANYBODY, ESPECIALLY A NOISY SEVEN YEAR OLD BOY WHO WOULD SURELY BREAK THIS WONDERFUL EXPERIENCE THAT I WAS HAVING EVERY MORNING. I HAD TO FIGHT THE TEMPTATION TO LET MARK SLEEP AND SNEAK OUT TO MY QUIET WORLD ALONE. BUT A PROMISE WAS A PROMISE.

SUPRISINGLY, USUALLY A SOUND SLEEPER, MARK BECAME WIDE AWAKE AT MY FIRST LIGHT TOUCH. AFTER SLIPPING INTO OUR CLOTHES AND DOWNING A QUICK BREAKFAST WE GATHERED UP OUR FISHING GEAR AND MADE OUR WAY DOWN TO THE BOAT LANDING.

WITH MARK SEATED SAFELY ON THE FRONT SEAT OF THE BOAT, WE SHOVED OFF. THE DECISION WAS MADE TO TROLL FOR A WHILE, AS THAT TAKES THE LEAST AMOUNT OF EFFORT AND WITH THE MOTOR THROTTLED WAY DOWN WE WOULDN'T BE BOTHERING ANYBODY AT THIS TIME OF THE MORNING. I AFFIXED THE BAIT TO OUR LINES, PUT MARKS ROD IN HIS HANDS, TOOK UP MY OWN AND WE WERE OFF.

BY SIX O'CLOCK WE HAD WORKED OUR WAY ABOUT HALF WAY AROUND THE LAKE. THIS PUT US ALONG AN UNINHABITED AREA OF BEACH WITH A HEAVY GROWTH OF WOODS BEHIND IT. THERE ARE NO ROADS, OR COTTAGES HERE WHICH MAKES IT MY FAVORITE SPOT. I WANTED TO LINGER HERE FOR AT LEAST A LITTLE WHILE. I SHUT OFF THE MOTOR AND UNDER THE PRETENSE OF BREAKING UP THE ROUTINE, TOLD MARK THAT WE WOULD BAIT-CAST FOR A WHILE.

WE WERE LAYING ABOUT TWENTY FEET OFF SHORE AND I WAS MAKING QUIET CASTS ALONG THE SHORELINE TRYING TO MAKE MY RETRIVES VARIED AND ATTRACTIVE TO ONE OF THE LARGER FISH THAT CAME IN TO THE SHALLOW WATERS EARLY IN THE MORNING TO FEED ON THE SMALLER FISH.

MARK WAS JUST PLOPPING HIS LURE ABOUT THREE BOAT LENGTHS OUT, LEAVING IT LAY THERE A BIT AND THEN SLOWLY REELING IT IN. AFTER HE HAD MADE A FEW CASTS I NOTICED THAT HE WAS CASTING INTO THE

SAME SPOT TIME AFTER TIME AND MENTIONED THAT MAYBE HE SHOULD TRY ANOTHER AREA. HE SAID THAT HE WAS TRYING TO HIT THE CENTER OF THE CIRCLE MADE BY THE RIPPLES ON THE CALM WATER. AFTER MAKING A COUPLE MORE CAST AS HE WAS REELING IN HIS LINE IT SUDDENLY WENT TAUNT.

I ADMONISHED HIM FOR LETTING HIS LINE SINK TO THE BOTTOM AND THEN DRAGGING IT ALONG THE ROCKS AND SUBMERGED LOGS AND BRANCHES AND GETTING A SNAG. I TOLD HIM TO KEEP THE SLACK OUT OF THE LINE SO IT WOULD NOT GET INTANGLED ONTO ANYTHING ELSE AND I'D TRY TO MANEUVER THE BOAT AROUND SO THAT WE COULD UNTANGLE THE SNAG.

I CIRCLED THE BOAT TO THE OTHER SIDE OF THE SNAG AND MARK TRIED WITH LITTLE JERKS AND SIDEWAYS PULLS TO GET HIS LINE FREE THAT DIDN'T WORK. FINALLY HE HANDED ME HIS ROD AND I TRIED EVERY WAY THAT HAD WORKED FOR ME IN THE PAST BUT TO NOT AVAIL.

IT LOOKED LIKE I WAS GOING TO HAVE TO CUT THE LINE AND RERIG IT. I TRIED ONE LAST SLINGSHOT ACTION WITH THE ROD AND THIS TIME IT FELT LIKE THE SNAG HAD PULLED BACK. I LOOKED OVER AT THE SHORELINE AND INSTEAD OF THE BOAT HOLDING STEADY OR DRIFTING BACK A LITTLE, IT HAD ACTUALLY MOVED SEVERAL FEET TOWARD THE SNAG. I GAVE THE LINE A

GOOD HARD STEADY PULL, THE SNAG GAVE ME TWO PULLS BACK.

I HANDED THE ROD BACK TO MARK AND SAID, SON, THAT SNAG IS PULLING BACK, IT'S ON YOUR LINE SO YOU'RE GOING TO HAVE TO DEAL WITH IT.

MARK SAT THERE LOOKING AT ME, NOT UNDERSTANDING. THIS ONLY LASTED FOR AN INSTANT WHEN HE FELT TREMENDOUS SERGE ON HIS POLE AS THE FISH STARTED A RUN.

HIS FISHING ROD WAS ALMOST JERKED OUT OF MARKS HAND, HE QUICKLY GRABBED IT WITH BOTH HANDS AND HELD ON.

I TOLD HIM TO LET THE FISH MAKE HIS RUN BUT TO KEEP THE SLACK OUT OF THE LINE, TO JUST PUT A LITTLE DRAG ON IT.

WHEN THE FISH FINALLY STOPPED, MARK SLOWLY BEGAN TO REEL HIM IN. ABOUT TEN FEET FROM THE BOAT, THE FISH TOOK OFF ON ANOTHER RUN.

MARK LOOKED AT ME, I SAID, IT'S ALRIGHT, THE FISH HAS FOUND ENOUGH STRENGTH FOR ANOTHER RUN, HE'S A HEALTY ONE. JUST KEEP DOING WHAT YOU'VE BEEN DOING. IT'S BETWEEN YOU AND HIM NOW. RIGHT THEN IT SEEMED THAT I WAS NO LONGER THERE. MARK

WAS THE ONLY ONE IN THE BOAT. MARKS FOCUS WAS COMPLETELY ON THE FISH.

THIS WAS HIS FIRST EXPERIENCE WITH A FIGHTING FISH AND HE DIDN'T NEED ME ANYMORE.

WITH THAT SECOND RUN THE FISH HAD USED UP THE LAST OF HIS ENERGY AND LOST, THIS TIME HE CAME EASILY UP TO THE BOAT. AT FIRST I THOUGHT THAT THE FISH MIGHT BE A PRETTY GOOD SIZE CATFISH BECAUSE OF ITS STRENGHT AND THE FACT THAT HE HAD BEEN AT THE BOTTOM OF THE LAKE. THEN AGAIN I THOUGHT THAT MAYBE IT WAS A NORTHERN PIKE BECAUSE OF THE WAY IT RAN. IT WAS A GREAT SURPRISE TO ME WHEN HE SURFACED AT THE BOAT. IT WAS NEITHER A NORTHERN OR A CATFISH. HE WAS A LARGE MOUTH BASS. I CALL HIM HE BECAUSE HE WASN'T POT-BELLIED WITH EGGS. HE WAS A BEAUTIFUL SLEEK BASS.

I QUICKLY NETTED THE FISH AND WHEN I BROUGHT HIM INTO THE BOAT HE SEEMED TO HALF FILL IT UP. WE ADMIRED HIM FOR A MINUTE OR TWO AND THEN I CRANKED UP THE OUTBOARD MOTOR AND HEADED STRAIGHT ACROSS THE LAKE FOR OUR DOCK, MOTOR WIDE OPENED. I PUT THE BASS ON A LONG STRINGER AND TIED HIM TO THE DOCK. SOME PEOPLE HAD SEEN US PULL UP TO THE DOCK WITH THE FISH AND WANTED TO GET A BETTER LOOK AT IT. MARK SPENT THE NEXT TWO HOURS TAKING THE BASS OUT OF THE WATER AND SHOWING IT AND THEN PUTTING IT BACK IN THE WATER.

THE WORD HAD GOTTEN AROUND ABOUT MARK AND HIS FISH AND SOME PICTURES WERE TAKEN. MARK GOT A LOT OF MILEAGE OUT OF HIS FISH THAT MORNING. I THOUGHT THAT HE WOULD SURELY WEAR THE POOR FISH COMPLETELY OUT WITH THE EXERCISE THAT MARK WAS GIVING IT. I'M CERTAIN THAT THE BASS LOST SOME WEIGHT.

AFTER LUNCH, ON THE ADVICE OF OUR RESORT OWNER, WE TOOK THE BASS INTO THE TOWN OF WALKER. THE BAIT SHOP THERE RAN AN ANNUAL FISHING CONTEST. IT WAS JUDGED IN AGE BRACKETS AND THE DIFFERENT FISH GROUPS. THE BASS WOULDN'T FIT IN A BUCKET, SO I CARRIED IT ON A STRINGER. WE HAD TO PARK A WAYS UP THE STREET FROM THE BAIT SHOP AND PEOPLE KEPT STOPPING US, SO AS TO GET A LOOK AT THE FISH, THEY ASKED US WHERE IT WAS CAUGHT AND WHAT BAIT WAS USED.

THE PEOPLE IN THE SHOP WERE VERY NICE. THEY SAID WHAT A WONDERFUL SPECIMEN OF A BASS IT WAS. THEN THEY WEIGHED AND MEASURED IT. IT WEIGHED SIX POUNDS, ELEVEN OUNCES AND WAS TWENTY ONE INCHES LONG. NEXT THEY ASKED MARKS NAME, AGE AND OUR ADDRESS. WE LET MARK ANSWER ALL THE QUESTIONS HIMSELF. WITH OUR PERMISSION, THEY FROZE THE FISH AND DISPLAYED IT IN THEIR BIG FRONT WINDOW ALONG WITH OTHER PRIZE FISH OF MANY TYPES. THE WHOLE WINDOW WAS A WONDERFUL DISPLAY OF FISH. THE PUBLIC, I SUPPOSE MOSTLY TOURIST,

SPENT MUCH TIME GAWKING THERE AND TALKING, IN LOW TONES, ABOUT THE VARIOUS FISH. WE MADE THE TRIP INTO WALKER EVERY DAY TO VISIT MR. BASS, HE REMAINED THE CENTER OF OUR ATTENTION FOR THE REST OF OUR VACATION. IT WAS A REAL THRILL TO STAND ON THE SIDEWALK IN FRONT OF THE BAIT-SHOP WINDOW AND SEE PEOPLE ADMIRING AND TALKING ABOUT MARKS FISH. IT WAS A GREAT EFFORT FOR ME NOT TO TELL THEM WHO'S FISH IT WAS.

BEFORE WE LEFT FOR HOME, THE LOCAL NEWSPAPER INTERVIEWED MARK AND TOOK HIS PICTURE. IT MUST HAVE BEEN A REAL HIGH FOR A SEVEN YEAR OLD BOY TO GET ALL THE ATTENTION THAT HE RECEIVED. SEVERAL WEEKS AFTER WE GOT HOME FROM OUR VACATION A PACKEAGE ARRIVED, ADRESSED TO MARK FROM WALKER, MINN. THE PACKAGE CONTAINED AN ASSORTMENT OF FISHING TACKLE AND ANNOUNCEMENT THAT MARK HAD WON THE CONTEST IN HIS AGE GROUP.

THE FISHING TRIP WAS RELIVED, ESPECIALLY THE MORNING OF MR. BASS, AND I THOUGHT TO MYSELF THAT MY "QUIET WORLD" HADN'T BEEN INVADED OR BROKEN INTO, MERELY SHARED WITH A NEW FISHING PAL......

A LONG DAY

IT WAS THE START OF ANOTHER DAY IN CHICAGO. AT 6 A.M. IT WAS STILL FAIRLY COOL BUT THAT WOULD GRADUALLY CHANGE WITH THE SLOWLY RISING SUN IN THE EAST. ENJOY THE EARLY MORNING BECAUSE THE CITY WOULD BECOME LIKE THE INSIDE OF A BAKE OVEN FROM ABOUT TEN IN THE MORNING UNTIL WELL INTO THE NIGHT. IT WAS THE MIDDLE OF JULY, 1980.

I WAS THE ENGINEER OF A FIVE MAN RAILROAD CREW. OUR JOB WAS TO HAUL MADE-UP FREIGHT TRAINS FROM OUR TRAIN YARDS TO VARIOUS RAIL YARDS OF DIFFERENT RAILROADS IN THE AREA WHERE THEY WOULD BE REMADE UP AND HAULED TO YARDS AROUND THE COUNTRY.

WE WENT TO WORK AT 7 P.M. AND TRANSFERRED AS MANY TRAINS AS WE COULD TO THE OTHER YARDS BEFORE 7 A.M. AND GET BACK TO OUR STARTING POINT BY 7 O'CLOCK IN THE MORNING. WE WOULD BE OUTLAWED AFTER THAT TIME. THAT WAS THE TWELVE HOUR LAW THAT WOULDN'T ALLOW US TO WORK MORE THEN TWELVE HOURS.

IF WE WENT PAST 7 A.M. WE WOULD HAVE TO PULL INTO
THE NEAREST SIDING, OUR CONDUCTOR WOULD FIND A
TELEPHONE CALL BOX, WE DIDN'T HAVE PHONES ON THE
ENGINES OR CABOOSES IN THOSE DAYS, AND INFORM
OUR DISPATCHER WHERE WE WERE AND HE WOULD
SEND OUT A LONE ENGINE FROM THE ROUNDHOUSE
THAT WOULD PULL US HOME. AFTER PUTTING IN
TWELVE HOURS WORKING ALL NIGHT WE DIDN'T WANT
THIS TO HAPPEN, WE WANTED TO GET ON HOME, CLEAN
UP AND GET SOME SLEEP.

THAT PARTICULAR MORNING AT 6 A.M. WE WERE JUST
AN ENGINE AND CABOOSE DEADHEADING IT, MAKING
A RUN FOR OUR HOME BASE. IT WAS ABOUT A TWENTY
FIVE MINUTE TRIP FROM WHERE WE WERE, IF WE HAD
CLEAR SAILING ALL THE WAY. WE DIDN'T. WE GOT
FLAGGED DOWN AT 6.10 AT THE SANTA FE CROSSING BY
THE SIGNAL MAN THERE BECAUSE THERE WAS A SANTA
FE PASSENGER TRAIN DUE TO CROSS THERE IN TEN
MINUTES AND THEY HAD THE RIGHT OF WAY, SO WE
WOULD HAVE TO SIT AND WAIT FOR THEM TO CROSS
BEFORE WE COULD GO HOME.

WHILE WE WERE WAITING I LOOKED OUT MY SIDE
WINDOW AND DID A DOUBLE-TAKE. I COULDN'T
BELIEVE WHAT I WAS LOOKING AT, THERE SAT A DOG, A
LITTLE BIGGER THEN A PUPPY WITH AN OLD PANTS BELT
FASTENED AROUND ITS NECK. THE BELT WAS SECURED
TO THE WOODEN CROSS-TIES BY NAILS, RIGHT IN THE
MIDDLE OF THE EAST-BOUND TRACKS WHERE THE

PASSENGER TRAIN WOULD COME RACING THROUGH AT ANY MOMENT.

I TOLD MY FIREMAN TO WATCH FOR THE SIGNAL MANS FLAG AND ADDED AS I DROPPED OFF THE ENGINE, THAT I'D BE RIGHT BACK. I TROTTED OVER TO THE EASTBOUD TRACKS WONDERING WHAT CONDITION THE DOG WAS IN AND ALSO IF IT WAS A BITER.

AS I NEARED THE LITTLE DOG IT LOOKED TO BE IN FAIR SHAPE. IT WAS LOOKING UP AT ME AND WAGGING ITS TAIL. THAT WAS A GOOD FRIENDLY SIGN TO ME. I'D CHANCE IT, NO TIME TO WASTE. I TRIED TO PULL THE BELT LOOSE FROM THE CROSS-TIES, BUT NO CHANCE. IT HAD BEEN NAILED DOWN TIGHT. I LOOSENED THE BELT FROM AROUND THE DOGS NECK AND PICKED THE LITTLE FELLA UP AS GENTLY AS I COULD. IT KINDA RELAXED AND NESTLED IN MY ARMS.

THE RAILROAD WAS ELEVATED ABOUT TWELVE FEET ABOVE THE STREET LEVEL THROUGH THE NEIGHBORHOODS, SAFER FOR THE PUBLIC AND FASTER GOING FOR US. AS I STOOD UP I NOTICED EIGHT OR TEN BOYS OF ABOUT TEN TO TWELVE YEARS OF AGE STANDING DOWN IN THE STREET, LOOKING UP AT ME. ONE OF THEM SPOKE UP AND HOLLERED, THAT'S MY DOG. I ANSWERED BACK, NOT ANYMORE IT ISN'T. AS I TURNED AND STARTED WALKING BACK TO THE ENGINE, I HEARD THE SAME BOY HOLLER AGAIN, YOU CAN'T TAKE MY DOG.

I TURNED MY HEAD AND SHOUTED OVER MY SHOULDER, WATCH ME. THIS TIME HE STEPPED FORWARD AND SAID, WE'LL COME UP THERE AND BEAT YOU UP.

BY THIS TIME I WAS AGITATED AND QUITE ANGRY, TO SAY THE LEAST. I TURNED BACK AROUND FACING THEM. I SQUARED MY SHOULDERS AND LOOKING AT ALL OF THEM SAID, IF ANY OF YOU BOYS WANT TO COME UP HERE, I'LL GLADLY KICK YOUR BUTTS FOR YOU AND SEND YOU HOME WHERE YOU BELONG. NONE OF THEM MOVED.

THE BOY THAT SAID THAT HE OWNED THE DOG WASN'T THROUGH YET, HE ANGERLY HOLLERED IN A LOUD VOICE, I'LL TELL MY DAD. IN AN EVEN LOUDER VOICE I SAID, I HOPE YOU DO AND BE SURE TO TELL HIM WHAT YOU AND YOUR FRIENDS TRIED TO DO HERE TODAY. THERE WAS COMPLETE SILENCE FOR A MINUTE OR TWO SO I TURNED AND WALKED TOWARD MY ENGINE. AS I WALKED I HEARD THE TWO TOOTS OF THE ENGINE THAT TOLD ME IT WAS CLEAR FOR US TO GO. BACK ON THE ENGINE I TOLD MY FIREMAN BILLY TO TAKE OVER AND RUN THE ENGINE HOME, THE LITTLE DOG WAS ASLEEP AND I DIDN'T WANT TO DISTURB IT.

AS WE STARTED TO MOVE BILLY SAID, HE'S AWFUL SMALL AND DIRTY. I ANSWERED, YES IT IS. SO DIRTY THAT IT'S HARD TO TELL IF IT'S COAT IS BROWN AND WHITE OR BROWN AND GREY, AND BY THE WAY, IT'S A SHE.

119

BILLY LOOKED OVER AT ME WITH WIDE EYES AND A SURPRISED EXPRESSION ON HIS FACE AND SAID, A LITTLE GIRL DOG, THAT MAKES THIS EVEN SADDER. WHAT ARE WE GOING TO DO?

WELL I SAID, WHENWE GET IN AND GET THE ENGINE AND CABOOSE PUT AWAY, WE'LL GO INTO THE LOCKER ROOM AND I'LL FILL OUT THE TIME SLIP AND YOU'LL HOLD THE PUP.

THEN WHAT? I MEAN LATER.

THEN I'LL TAKE THE LITTLE GIRL HOME WITH ME. AND MY WIFE JAN, WILL WANT TO TAKE CHARGE. WE'LL GIVE HER SOME WATER AND FEED HER A LITTLE AND GIVE HER A BATH. LATER I'LL TAKE HER OVER TO THE VET CLINIC AND HAVE THE DOC CHECK HER OVER TO SEE WHAT CONDITION SHE'S IN. HE MAY GIVE HER SOME SHOTS AND WORK OUT A DIET FOR HER. NEXT, I'LL TAKE HER HOME, JAN WILL TAKE CARE OF HER WHILE I GET SOME SLEEP.

ARE YOU GOING TO KEEP HER?

CAN'T. WE'VE ALREADY GOT THREE DOGS AND THAT'S ALL YOU CAN HAVE IN OUR AREA. WE'LL GET HER SETTLED AND FIND HER A GOOD HOME. IT MAY TAKE A WHILE.

THAT SOUNDS LIKE A GOOD PLAN.

IT'S THE ONLY THING THAT CAN BE DONE. THIS LITTLE DOG NEEDS HELP, SHE DESERVES SOME KINDNESS AND RIGHT NOW IT LOOKS LIKE I'VE BEEN ELECTED.

THAT'S SWELL OF YOU.

IT NEEDS TO BE DONE. HAS TO BE DONE.

WE GOT INTO THE LOCKER ROOM WITH EIGHT MINUTES TO SPARE. WHILE I WAS FILLING OUT THE TIMESLIP, JACK TRUMBLE, THE DAY SHIPPING CLERK CAME INTO THE ROOM. HE NOTICED THE PUP IN BILLYS ARMS AND SAID, THAT'S A CUTE LITTLE PUPPY.

BILLY COMMENTED, SHE'S A GIRL PUP AND VERY DIRTY. THEN HE EXPLAINED TO JACK HOW WE HAD FOUND HER.

JACK FROWNED AND SAID, KIDS CAN BE VERY CRUEL SOMETIMES. HE WENT ON TO SAY, MY WIFE AND I ARE THINKING ABOUT GETTING A DOG. HE LEANED OVER AND WHISPERED TO ME. WE CAN'T HAVE KIDS. JACK WAS IN HIS EARLY THIRTIES. HW WAS CALM AND LEVEL HEADED.

I ASKED HIM WHERE HE LIVED AND IF HE HAD A FENCED IN BACK YARD AND IF HIS WIFE WORKED.

JACK ANSWERED, MY WIFE HAZEL AND I LIVE IN THE MARQUETTE PARK AREA IN A VERY NICE BUNGALOW. MY GRANDFATHER LEFT ME SOME MONEY AND WE WERE

ABLE TO PAY CASH FOR THE HOUSE AND THE FURNITURE. YES WE HAD A FENCED IN BACK YARD, IT'S MOSTLY GRASS AND QUITE LARGE AND NO MY WIFE DOESN'T WORK. SHE'S A HOSEWIFE AND THAT'S THE WAY WE BOTH LIKE IT. ANY OTHER QUESTIONS?

NO, I TOLD HIM WHAT I WAS GOING TO DO WITH THE PUP AFTER WORK AND SAID THAT TOMORROW IS SATURDAY AND IF YOU AND YOUR WIFE WOULD BE INTERESTED IN SEEING THE PUP AFTER SHE'S CLEANED UP, MY WIFE JAN AND I COULD BRING HER OVER TO YOUR HOUSE JUST TO LOOK AT. SAY BETWEEN 9 AND 10 O'CLOCK. JACK GOT A LITTLE EXCITED. WOULD YOU DO THAT? YES! YES! 9 OR 10, WILL BE FINE. HE WROTE HIS ADDRESS ON A PIECE OF PAPER AND HANDED IT TO ME. WE'LL BE LOOKING FOR YOU AT 9 OR 10. THANK YOU.

NOW JACK, IT ALL DEPENDS ON WHAT THE VET HAS TO SAY ABOUT HER. SHE MAY HAVE SOMETHING WRONG WITH HER. KEEP AN OPEN MIND AND HOPE FOR THE BEST AND WE'LL SEE YOU IN THE MORNING. WE NEED HER TO HAVE A CLEAN BILL OF HEALTH.

WHEN I PULLED INTO THE DRIVE-WAY AT HOME, THERE SHE STOOD RIGHT IN THE MIDDLE OF HER FLOWER-BED WEARING THE SAME SMILE I WAS ALWAYS GREETED WITH WHEN I GOT HOME FROM WORK. NO MATTER WHAT MOOD I WAS IN OR HOW BAD A DAY I HAD HAD, IT GAVE ME A FEELING OF JOY JUST TO GAZE AT THAT LOVELY

SMILE AND KNOW THE BEAUTIFUL PERSON THAT WAS INSIDE HER.

SHE HOLLERED HI THERE STRANGER. I ANSWERED, HI YOURSELF. I PUT THE LITTLE DOG UNDER MY ARM AND STARTED UP THE WALK. JAN GAVE A HARD LOOK AND ASKED, HEY, WHAT'S THAT UNDER YOUR ARM?

I TRIED TO ACT SMOOTH. JUST A LITTLE SOMETHING I PICKED UP. WE MET AT THE FRONT DOOR AND JAN KINDA GRABBED THE PUP FROM UNDER MY ARM, LIFTED THE DOG UP ABOUT EYE HIGH AND SAID, WHAT HAVE WE HERE? THEY WERE BOTH LOOKING STRAIGHT INTO EACH OTHERS EYES AND I HAD THE FEELING THAT IT WAS LOVE AT FIRST SIGHT FOR BOTH OF THEM.

WITHOUT LOOKING AT ME, JAN GAVE THE COMMAND, GO SHOO OUR DOGS INTO THE BACK YARD. I GAVE A SNAPPY SALUTE AND SAID, AYE AYE SIR AND WENT INTO THE HOUSE.

I WAS IN THE LIVING ROOM AND THERE WERE OUR THREE DACHSHUNDS SPRAWLED OUT ON THE FLOOR IN DIFFERENT LOCATIONS. I SAID, GOOD MORNING GUYS, I SEE YOU'RE NOT PLAYING WATCHDOG THIS MORNING.

TWO OF THEM LIFTED THEIR HEAD UP A LITTLE AND LOOKED MY WAY, THEN EASED THEM DOWN AGAIN. I CLEARED MY THROAT AND SAID IN A LOUD VOICE, WE'RE GOING OUT TO THE BACK YARD. O.K.?

THEY WERE ALL FULLY AWAKE NOW AND JUMPED UP AND FOLLOWED ME THROUGH THE HOUSE. WHILE GOING THROUGH THE KITCHEN, WITHOUT STOPPING I STOOPED OVER AND PICKED UP THEIR WATERBOWL AND THEN WENT AND OPENED THE BACK DOOR. THEY ALL BOUNCED INTO THE BACKYARD AND DISPERSED IN DIFFERENT DIRECTIONS, SNIFFING THE GROUND AS THEY MADE THEIR WAY ACROSS THE GRASS. I SET THE WATERBOWL NEXT TO THE DOOR AND WALKED OVER TO THE STORAGE SHED. WHERE I GOT OUT THE ROUND WASHTUB AND LAID IT DOWN NEXT TO THE GARDEN HOSE AND RAN ABOUT THREE INCHES OF WATER INTO IT, AFTER THAT I WENT BACK INTO THE KITCHEN.

JAN HAD GOTTEN OUT ANOTHER BOWL AND HALF FILLED IT WITH WATER. THE LITTLE DOG STARTED DRINKING AND DIDN'T STOP. AFTER SHE HAD DRANK ABOUT HALF THE WATER. JAN PULLED THE PUPS FACE OUT THE WATER AND SET THE BOWL UP ON THE COUNTER AND PUT THE BOWL OF DRY DOG FOOD IN FRONT OF THE PUP. SHE TOOK ONE SNIFF AND DIVED IN AND STARTED EATING AS THOUGH SHE HADN'T HAD ANY FOOD IN A WEEK. IN A WHILE JAN PICKED UP THE BOWL AND SAID WHOA, SHE PUT IT ON THE COUNTER WITH THE OTHER ONE, THE LITTLE DOG LOOKED UP AT JAN WITH PLEADING EYES. JAN SAID TO HER, I KNOW YOU NEED MORE, WE'LL SEE HOW THAT MUCH SETS WITH YOU AND GIVE YOU SOME MORE LATER. WHILE THIS WAS ON I WAS BUSY FILLING FOUR LARGE POTS AND PANS WITH WATER AND PUTTING THEM ON THE KITCHEN

STOVE AND TURNING ON THE BURNERS, JAN LOOKED AT ME AND ASKED, OK YOU, WHAT'S THE STORY? WHERE DID YOU FIND THIS LITTLE ORPHAN?

WHILE THE WATER WAS HEATING I TOLD HER THE WHOLE STORY. THEN I WENT ON WITH THE NEXT STORY. I GOT OUT THE BIG WASH TUB AND PUT A LITTLE WATER FROM THE HOSE IN IT. NOW I'M HEATING THIS WATER SO WE CAN ADD IT TO THE TUB AND YOU CAN GIVE BABY THERE A NICE LONG WARM BATH WHILE I GO TO THE HARDWARE STORE AND GET SOME THINGS.

WHAT SORT OF THINGS?

OH. A LITTLE DOGGY BED, A COLLAR AND LEASH, HER OWN WATER AND FOOD BOWLS AND ANYTHING ELSE I CAN THINK OF THAT SHE MIGHT NEED. NEXT WE'LL TAKE HER OVER TO THE VETERINARY CLINIC WHERE THE VET WILL CHECK HER OVER AND MAYBE GIVE HER SOME SHOTS. THEN WE'LL ALL GO OUT TO THE BACK YARD AND LOUNGE AROUND IN THE SHADE AND MAYBE TAKE A LITTLE NAP.

YOU'RE REALLY GOOD AT PLANNING.

I KNOW, I KNOW…. HE! HE!

WHEN I GOT HOME FROM THE STORE JAN WAS SITTING ON THE GRASS WITH A BIG OLD BATH TOWEL IN HER LAP WITH THE PUPPY LAYING ON HER BACK IN THE MIDDLE

OF THE TOWEL. JAN WAS GENTLY DRYING THE LITTLE DOGS TUMMY. OUR THREE DOGS WERE UP CLOSE, WATCHING THE WHOLE PROCEEDINGS. GRETCHEN, OUR OLDEST DOG EASED RIGHT UP TO THE PUP AND SNIFFED HER. THE OTHER TWO DOGS DID THE SAME. THEN ALL THREE BACKED OFF. I SAID, LOOKS LIKE THEY'RE EXCEPTING HER INTO THE FAMILY.

YES I THINK THEY ARE. WHEN WE BRING HER BACK FROM THE VET IF SHE'S HEALTHY, WE'LL PUT ALL THE DOGS IN THE BACK YARD, AND SEE WHAT HAPPENS. IF IT WORKS OK THIS EVENING WE'LL FEED THEM TOGETHER AND TONIGHT WE'LL CLOSE BABY IN THE KITCHEN. WITH HER BED AND A BOWL OF WATER THERE SHE'LL FEEL SAFE.

NOW WHO'S THE BIG PLANNER?

WELL. DOESN'T THAT SOUND RIGHT?

YES IT DOES AND DON'T FORGET, IN THE MORNING WE TAKE HER OVER TO JACK AND HAZEL'S PLACE.

SUPPOSE THEY DON'T HAVE A NICE YARD OR THEY WANT TO MAKE HER AN OUTSIDE DOG OR IF THEY DON'T WANT HER?

THEN WE BRING HER BACK HERE AND LOOK FOR OTHER GOOD PEOPLE TO TAKE HER.

ISN'T THERE SOME WAY WE CAN KEEP HER? SHE NEEDS SAFETY.

YOU KNOW THE RULES. THREE DOGS MAX. WE'LL MAKE SURE SHE ENDS UP IN AN IDEAL HOME.

IF ANYBODY ASKS, WE COULD BE TAKING CARE OF HER FOR PEOPLE WHO ARE ON A LONG TRIP.

JAN...OH...A... WHY DO YOU ALWAYS HAVE TO BE SO RIGHT?

I DON'T KNOW. MAYBE IT'S BUILT INTO ME. REMEMBER, YOU TOOK ME FOR BETTER OR FOR WORST. YOU'RE KINDA STUCK WITH ME...

I CAN HANDLE IT.

JAN PLANS ALL WORKED OUT THAT EVENING AND NIGHT. WE PUT THE PUPS BED IN THE CORNER NEXT TO THE STOVE AND JAN TOOK HER TO IT. THE LITTLE DOG CLIMBED INTO HER BED MADE A COUPLE OF CIRCLES AND LAYED DOWN. WE BLOCKED THE DOORWAY INTO THE REST OF THE HOUSE WITH A DOGGY GATE. THE LITTLE DOG DIDN'T CRY OR MAKE ANY SOUNDS WHEN WE TURNED THE OVERHEAD LIGHTS OFF IN THE KITCHEN. WE LEFT A SMALL LIGHT OVER THE STOVE ON IN CASE SHE GOT THIRSTY DURING THE NIGHT. SHE COULD FIND HER WATER BOWL.

THE OTHER DOGS LOOKED THROUGH THE GATE FOR A SHORT WHILE AND THEN WENT TO THEIR OWN BEDS FOR THE NIGHT.

IN THE MORNING WHEN WE LOOKED IN THE KITCHEN, THERE WAS THE LITTLE DOG LAYING IN HER BED LOOKING AT US. SHE HAD SETTLED IN AND MADE HERSELFT AT HOME, I GUESS THAT SHE FELT HERSELF ALREADY PART OF THE FAMILY.

AT ABOUT EIGHT THIRTY I LOADED THE PUPS BED AND DISHES INTO THE TRUNK OF THE CAR, JAN TOOK THE DOG INTO THE BACK SEAT AND SAT WITH HER ARM AROUND HER AND SPOKE TO HER IN SOFT TONES. THE PUP LAYED THERE QUIETLY, LISTENING.

I DROVE OVER TO THE MARQUETTE PARK NEIGHBORHOOD AND FOUND JACKS STREET. THE STREET WAS TREE LINED WITH WELL KEPT FRONT YARDS, NO CLUTTER ANYWHERE AND QUIET. ALL THE HOMES WERE OF BRICK CONTRUCTION.

WE FOUND JACKS HOUSE, WENT UP ON THE PORCH AND RANG THE DOORBELL. JACK OPENED THE DOOR ALMOST IMMEDIATELY AND SAID, YOU FOUND US, GOOD MORNING, COME IN. COME IN. I SAID, GOOD MORNING JACK, I WONDER IF WE CAN SEE YOUR BACKYARD.

BACKYARD? OH I SEE. YES, FOLLOW ME.

JACK LED US AROUND THE HOUSE AND BACK TO A WELL CONSTRUCTED GATE AND INTO THE YARD WHICH WAS INDEED QUITE LARGE WITH A LOT OF GRASS AND A GOOD FENCE AS JACK HAD TOLD ME THE DAY BEFORE. EVERYTHING WAS PERFECT SO FAR. WE WENT UP ON A NICE BIG PORCH THAT HELD SEVERAL CHAIRS AND A TABLE.

WE SAT DOWN AND JACK ASKED IF WE'D LIKE SOME COFFEE.

JAN ANSWERED, THAT SOUNDS GOOD. SHE HAD THE DOG IN HER LAP. JACK WENT INTO THE HOUSE AND RETURNED IN A FEW MINUTES CARRYING A TRAY WITH THE COFFEE THINGS ON IT FOLLOWED BY A LADY, WHO JACK INTRODUCED TO US AS HIS WIFE, HAZEL.

JACK SAID THAT PUPPY LOOKS A LOT DIFFERENT THEN WHEN I SAW IT YESTERDAY.

I LAUGHED AND SAID YES, NOW WE KNOW FOR SURE THAT SHE'S WHITE WITH BROWN SPOTS. SHE GOT A CLEAN BILL OF HEALTH FROM THE VET AND FROM THE SHAPE OF HER HEAD AND EARS AND HER SMALL BODY AND FEET, I'D GUESS THAT SHE'S MOSTLY BEAGLE.

DID SHE FUSS MUCH LAST NIGHT?

NOT AT ALL. SHE WAS VERY PATIENT AT THE VETS AND SETTLED IN NICELY AT OUR HOUSE. NOT A PEEP OUT OF HER DURING THE NIGHT.

JACK SAID, I THINK SHE'S KINDA PRETTY.

WE ALL AGREED.

HAZEL HAD BEEN TALKING WITH US, GETTING AQUAINTED, BUT HER EYES NEVER LEFT THE LITTLE DOG IN JANS LAP. FINALLY SHE ASKED JAN, MAY I HOLD HER?

JAN ANSWERED, OF COURSE. DON'T GET UP; I'LL BRING HER TO YOU.

HAZEL WAS SITTING WITH HER HANDS IN HER LAP.

JAN PLACED THE LITTLE DOG THERE.

THE PUP WIGGLED A LITTLE AND LAID HER CHIN ON HAZELS LEFT FOREARM.

WITH A MONA LIZA SMILE HAZEL BEGAN TO GENTLY STROKE THE PUPS BACK WITH HER RIGHT HAND.

I THINK THIS TOUCHED ALL OF US.

JAN AND I GAVE EACH OTHER A LOOK AND I HAD A STRONG FEELING THAT THE LITTLE ORPHAN HAD JUST FOUND A NEW HOME WITH TWO GOOD PEOPLE.

JACK ASKED, DOES SHE HAVE A NAME?

WE'VE ONLY KNOWN HER FOR A DAY. SHE MIGHT HAVE A NAME, WE'LL NEVER KNOW.

WHAT DO YOU THINK WOULD BE A GOOD NAME FOR HER?

WELL, SHE'S KINDA LAID BACK AND SEEMS TO BE COMFORTABLE WITH EVERYONE. I THINK SHE'S A DAISY OR A MOLLY.

WITHOUT TAKING HER EYES OFF OF THE LITTLE DOG, HAZEL SAID, SHE'S DEFINITLY A MOLLY.

JACK SAID. I AGREE.

WELL THEN MOLLY IT IS.

JACK RAISED HIS COFFEE CUP AND SAID TO MOLLY.

WE ALL JOINED JACK IN HIS TOAST.

AFTER A MINUTE OR TWO OF SILENCE I SPOKE UP. JAN AND I HAVE A DEAL FOR YOU TWO. YOU CAN SAY YES OR NO TO IT. THE DEAL IS THIS. WE CAN LEAVE MOLLY HERE WITH YOU FOR A DAY OR TWO, OR A WEEK OR TWO AS A TRAIL FOR YOU TO SEE IF YOU REALLY WANT A DOG LIVING IN YOUR HOUSE AND IF MOLLY IS THAT DOG. THERE'S GOING TO BE PROBLEMS AND ACCIDENTS. IT'S NOT ALL FUN. SO IS IT A YES OR NO?

HAZEL SAID, I THINK IT'S A FINE IDEA. NEITHER JACK NOR I HAVE EVER HAD A DOG.

JACK CHIPPED IN. SOUNDS FAIR TO ME.

DON'T HESITATE TO TELL US IF YOU FIND THAT YOU CAN'T HANDLE IT, WE WANT MOLLY TO HAVE A GOOD SAFE, HAPPY LIFE WITH A GOOD FAMILY AND WE'LL FIND A GOOD HOME FOR HER.

HAZEL, JAN CAN FILL YOU IN ON HOW TO TAKE CARE OF A DOG WHILE JACK AND I GET SOME THINGS FROM MY CAR.

WHEN JACK AND I GOT BACK TO THE PORCH WITH MOLLYS THINGS, THE GIRLS WERE NO LONGER THERE. WE FOUND THEM IN THE KITCHEN SITTING AT THE TABLE DRINKING COFFEE. JAN WAS TALKING AND HAZEL WAS TAKING NOTES ON A PAD OF PAPER.

I ASKED, WHERE DO YOU WANT THE BED?

JAN SPOKE UP, OVER IN THAT CORNER, NEXT TO THE FRIG.

JACK HELD UP THE TWO BOWELS, JAN SAID, NEAR THE BED BUT PUT SOME COLD WATER IN ONE OF THEM FIRST.

JAN REACHED INTO ONE OF THE PAPER BAGS AND PULLED OUT A SMALL BAG OF DRY DOG FOOD AND SAID, WE KEEP

SOME OF THIS IN A BOWL BY THE WATER DISH. YOU MAY WANT TO GET TWO MORE BOWLS. YOU SHOULD KEEP SOME WATER ON THE PORCH SO SHE'LL HAVE ACCESS TO WATER AT ALL TIMES, THAT'S VERY IMPORTANT. THE OTHER BOWL WILL BE FOR THE CANNED DOG FOOD THAT YOU'LL GIVE HER IN THE EVENING.

HAZEL WAS WRITING EVERY THING DOWN.

JAN NEXT PULLED OUT THE CAN OF PARTIALLY FILLED PUPPY FOOD THAT WE HAD OPENED THE NIGHT BEFORE, IT HAD A PLASTIC LID ON IN IT TO KEEP IT FRESH, WE KEEP THE OPENED CANS IN THE FRIG WE GAVE HER A THIRD OF THIS CAN YESTERDAY. YOU CAN GIVE HER HALF OF WHAT'S LEFT TONIGHT. WE FEED OUR DOGS AT ABOUT FIVE O'CLOCK, THAT WAY THEY DON'T HANG AROUND THE TABLE LOOKING FOR SOMETHING TO EAT WHILE WE'RE HAVING SUPPER. IF MOLLY LOOKS LIKE SHE'S LOSING WEIGHT YOU CAN UP IT TO HALF A CAN A DAY. AFTER A FEW WEEKS YOU CAN SWITCH FROM PUPPY TO REGULAR DOG FOOD. GET IT AT THE PET SHOP.

I LOOKED AT JAN AND ASKED, DID YOU TELL HAZEL THAT IT'S A GOOD IDEA TO TAKE MOLLY OUT THE FIRST THING IN THE MORNING AND THE LAST THINK IN THE EVENING?

YES I DID.

I PULLED OUT THE LEASH FROM THE OTHER SACK AND HELD IT UP THIS IS MOLLY'S LEASH. THIS SNAP FASTENS ONTO THE RING ON HER COLLAR WHICH GIVES ME ANOTHER IDEA, HAZEL. WHY DON'T YOU AND JAN TAKE MOLLY FOR A LITTLE WALK RIGHT NOW? IT'LL GIVE HER THE FEEL OF WALKING ON A LEASH AND LET HER GET A LOOK AT THE NEIGHBORHOOD.

HAZEL LOOKED AT JAN WHO SAID, LET'S GO.

AFTER THE GIRLS LEFT THE HOUSE WITH MOLLY JACK HELD OUT HIS HAND TO ME AND SAID, THANK YOU. WITH THREE OF US IN THE HOUSE IT'LL MAKE US SEEM MORE LIKE A FAMILY.

NOT SO FAST JACK. LIKE I SAID YESTERDAY, YOU AND HAZEL WILL HAVE TO KEEP OPEN MINDS ABOUT THIS. EVERYTHING IS NOT GOING TO BE A BED OF ROSES. THERE'LL BE TIMES WHEN YOU'LL BOTH HAVE DOUBTS ABOUT IT. BUT IN THE END, YES, IT'LL BE WORTH IT FOR BOTH OF YOU. REMEMBER THIS JACK, NO MATTER WHAT MOLLY DOES WRONG, NO HITTING AND NO SCREAMING OR SHOUTING. THESE ACTIONS WILL ONLY CONFUSE HER. YOU CAN USE A DIFFERENT VOICE, A STERN VOICE AND TALK TO HER. AFTER A FEW TIMES SHE'LL KNOW THAT WHAT SHE JUST DID WAS WRONG. YOU HAVE TO DO THIS IMMEDIATELY AFTER IT HAPPENS, WHAT I JUST SAID APPLIES TO CHILDREN ALSO. AND REMEMBER JACK, WHEN YOU HAVE ANY PROBLEMS OR QUESTIONS, CALL US.

WE'LL HELP YOU WORK THEM OUT.

WHEN THE GIRLS GOT BACK FROM THEIR WALK THEY WERE BOTH SMILING.

DID SOMEBODY TELL A JOKE I ASKED?

NO ANSWERED JAN, MOLLY WAS SO GOOD, YOU WOULDN'T BELIEVE IT. SHE WALKED ALONG WITH US WITHOUT PULLING OR TUGGING. SHE SNIFFED EVERYTHING. FIRST THE GRASS, THEN THE FLOWERS AND THE TREES AND DIDN'T SEEM TO BE AFRAID, JUST CURIOUS. I WAS TELLING HAZEL, IT'D BE GOOD FOR BOTH OF THEM TO WALK A COUPLE OF TIMES A DAY. JUST SHORT WALKS AT FIRST. I THINK FOR NOW THE KITCHEN SHOULD BE MOLLYS ROOM. THEY CAN PUT SOME KIND OF BARRIER ACROSS THE DOORWAY TO THE OTHER PART OF THE HOUSE. WITH HER BED AND WATER IN THE KITCHEN MOLLY WILL FEEL SAFE AND COMFORTABLE THERE. IF SHE HAS TO GO DURING THE NIGHT IT'LL BE EASIER TO CLEAN UP. AFTER A WEEK OR SO THEY CAN LEAVE THE DOORWAY OPEN AND SEE WHAT SHE DOES. I THINK SHE'LL CHOOSE THE KITCHEN.

ON THE DRIVE HOME I SAID, YESTERDAY WAS A VERY VERY LONG DAY BUT WELL WORTH IT. WE RESCUED A LITTLE ORPHAN AND FOUND A NICE HOME FOR HER WITH NICE PEOPLE, YEP. IT WAS A VERY HOT LONG DAY......

A VOICE IN THE COLONIES

AN ANCESTER OF MINE ANNE HUTCHINSON IS MY GREAT AUNT, ABOUT EIGHT OR NINE GENERATIONS REMOVED. SHE SAILED FROM ENGLAND WITH PART OF HER FAMILY IN THE EARLY 1600s. THEY WER BOUND FOR THE NEW WORLD, THE AMERICAN COLONIES FOR RELIGIOUS AND OTHER REASONS.

SHE WASN'T A TYPICAL HOUSEWIFE OF THE TIME. SHE DIDN'T STAY HOME AND PERFORM HER WIFELY DUTIES ALL HER WAKING HOURS AS THE ALL MALE RULING BODY OF THE TIME THOUGHT THAT THE WOMEN OF THE COMMUNITY SHOULD DO.

ALTHOUGH SHE HAD FOURTEEN CHILDREN, SHE FOUND THE TIME TO ATTEND TOWN MEETINGS AND CHURCH SERVICE AND ALSO HELD MEETINGS IN HER OWN HOME FOR THE WOMEN OF THE TOWN WHO WERE TOO BUSY AND TIRED TO GO TO THE REGULAR SERVICES. SHE SOMETIMES STOOD UP AT TOWN MEETINGS AND GAVE VOICE TO HER THOUGHTS AND OPINIONS ON THE STATE OF THINGS AND HOW SHE THOUGHT THEY COULD BE MADE BETTER. HER IDEAS WERE OFTEN CONTRARY TO

THE COUNCILS, WHICH WAS SUPPOSEDLY GOVERNED BY STRICT RULES AND BELIEFS.

HE SO CALLED, UNETHICAL BEHAVIOR CONFUSED AND ANGERED THE RULING BODY AND THE CHURCH OFFICALS, WHO WERE OFT-TIMES ONE AND THE SAME. THEY TRIED VARIOUS MEANS OF CONTAINING HER, BUT SHE REMAINED MOST VOCAL AND PERSISTANT AND WOULD NOT GIVE IN TO THE PRESSURES THEY PLACED UPON HER. SHE HAD MANY LOYAL FOLLOWERS NOT ONLY AMONG THE WOMEN. BUT ALSO SOME OF THE MEN IN THE AREA WERE STARTING TO TAKE HEED OF HER WORDS.

HER INFLUENCE WAS GROWING SO QUICKLY AND STRONG IN THE COMMUNITY THAT THE TOWN LEADERS DECIDED TO TAKE DRASTIC ACTION. THEY HELD HER TRIAL IN NOVEMBER OF 1637 IN CAMBRIDGE, MASSACHUSETTS. SHE WAS CONVICTED OF HERESY AND CONTEMPT, EXCOMMUNICATED BY THE BOSTON CHURCH AND BANISHED FROM MASSACHUSETTS.

WHEN SHE ASKED THE REASON FOR HER PUNISHMENT SHE WAS TOLD THAT THE COURT KNOWS BEST AND IS SATISFIED. SHE WASN'T EVEN ALLOWED TO DEFEND HERSELF. THE FOLLOWING YEAR WITH HER FAMILY AND SMALL GROUP OF FOLLOWERS, SHE SETTLED AT POCASSET. (NOW KNOWN AS PORTSMOUTH, R. I.).

THERE THEY PURCHASED LAND FROM THE INDIANS AND FOUNDED THE COLONY OF RHODE ISLAND. EVEN THOUGH SHE WAS CONFINED TO RHODE ISLAND AND LATER PELHAM BAY, NEW YORK, SHE DIDN'T GIVE UP HER CAUSES. HER WORDS AND INFLUENCE WERE HEARD AND FELT THROUGHOUT ALL OF THE COLONIES. MANY WONDERED WHAT EFFECT SHE WOULD HAVE ON THE FUTURE OF THE COLONIES.

IN THE FALL OF 1643, I'M SURE THAT A GREAT SIGH OF RELIEF WAS EXPELLED THROUGHTOUT THE COLONIES BY CIVIL AS WELL AS CHURCH OFFICALS AND OTHERS. IT WAS LEARNED THAT ANNE HUTCHINSON AND MOST OF HER FAMILY HAD BEEN MURDERED BY WHAT WAS THOUGHT OF AS FRIENDLY INDIANS IN A MASSACRE.

NOW THE LEADERS OF THE COLONIES COULD GO BACK TO RULING AND CONTROLLING THINGS AND EVERYTING WOULD BE BACK AS IT SHOULD BE, AS THEY FIGURED THAT GOD HAD PLANNED IT TO BE, AND IT SOON WAS.

THROUGH THE GENERATIONS TO FOLLOW, THE HUTCHINSON DESCENDENTS HAVE LIVED FAIRLY NORMAL LIVES, NO REBLES WITH CAUSES AND NO RELIGIOUS ZEALOTS.

ALTHOUGH WE HAVE SERVED AND BEEN REPRESENTED IN JUST ABOUT EVERY CONFLICT AND WAR THAT AMERICA HAS BEEN INVOLVED IN, WE'VE BECOME QUITE

PASSIVE. WE DON'T STAND UP AND VOICE OUR OPINIONS AT MEETINGS ANYMORE.

GREAT AUNT, ANNE HUTCHINSONS BLOOD HAS GROWN THIN IN OUR VEINS AND WE HAVE BECOME MERELY, CITIZENS OF THE UNITED STATES OF AMERICA......

A QUIET TRIBUTE

MISTER ELI M. HUTCHINSON WAS BORN IN UPPER NEW YORK STATE JUNE 7TH 1838. HE WAS A DIRECT DECENDENT OF ANNE HUTCHINSON, A RELIGIOUS LEADER IN AMERICA IN THE EARLY 1600s. HE WAS ALSO MY GREAT GRANFATHER. WHEN HE WAS 16 HE MOVED WITH HIS PARENTS FROM NEW YORK STATE TO NORA SPRINGS, IOWA, WHICH WAS A SMALL FARMING COMMUNITY IN NORTH CENTRAL IOWA.

ELI WAS 23 YEARS OLD WHEN THE CIVIL WAR BEGAN. IN 1863 HE ENLISTED IN THE UNION ARMY WITH COMPANY K OF THE IOWA 27TH AT OSAGE IOWA. HE SAW ACTION IN FIVE BATTLES INCLUDING VICKSBURG, PLEASANT HILL, FRANKLIN, MOBILE AND IN THE RED RIVER CAMPAIGN HE WAS UNDER FIRE FOR 90 STRAIGHT DAYS. HE WAS DISCHARGED FROM THE ARMY IN DECEMBER, 1865 AT DAVENPORT, IOWA AND RETURNED TO NORA SPRINGS.

ELI FARMED TO SOME EXTENT, BUT SPENT MOST OF HIS TIME AS A CARPENTER, A TRADE THAT HIS FATHER HAD FOLLOWED BEFORE HIM. ELI BUILT LOG CABINS, FARM BUILDINGS AND MANY OF THE HOMES IN AND AROUND

NORA SPRINGS. HE BUILT A SAWMILL AND A GRIST MILL. HE BUILT THE OLD MILL AT ROCK CREEK AND ALSO A ONE ROOM SCHOOL HOUSE THERE. THE FIRST TEACHER OF THE SCHOOL WAS MISS MARY DUDLEY, WHO WAS TO BECOME ELI'S WIFE IN 1866. THE SCHOOL WAS EVER AFTER KNOWN AS THE DUDLEY SCHOOL.

IN 1900 GREAT GRANDFATHER ELI DECIDED TO RETIRE FROM CARPENTRY TRADE AT THE AGE OF 62. HE THEN APPLIED FOR A JOB WITH THE UNITED STATES POSTAL SERVICE AND WAS GIVEN THE HONOR OF BECOMING THE FIRST RURAL MAIL CARRIER IN THE NORA SPRINGS DISTRICT. HE WORKED AT THIS JOB FOR THE NEXT 20 YEARS AND AT THE AGE OF 82 FINALLY RETIRED FOR GOOD.

MY FAMILY LIVED IN CHICAGO, ILLINOIS THROUGH ALL OF MY GROWING UP YEARS. WHILE MY SISTER AND I WERE GROWING UP BOTH OF OUR PARENTS WORKED MOST OF THE TIME, SO WE WERE LATCHKEY KIDS FOR ALL OF OUR SCHOOL YEARS. THERE WERE RULES FOR US TO FOLLOW AND WE GOT INTO ROUTINES THAT MADE IT FAIRLY EASY TO DO SO. IN THE SUMMERS WE WOULD GO TO IOWA AND SPEND SEVERAL WEEKS THERE VISITING WITH OUR GRANDPARENTS. TRAVELING EITHER BY TRAIN OR AUTO, IT WAS A TRIP OF ABOUT 350 MILES. WE WOULD DIVIDE OUR TIME BETWEEN MY FATHERS PARENTS IN ROCKFORD IOWA, ANOTHER SMALL FARMING TOWN AND NORA SPRINGS. THE TOWNS WERE SET APART BY ABOUT TWELVE MILES.

I WAS FIVE YEARS OLD WHEN MY GRANDMOTHER ELIZABETH WHO LIVED IN NORA SPRINGS, FIRST TOOK ME TO VISIT MY GREAT GRANDPARENTS. IT WAS JUST A SHORT WALK FROM HER HOUSE TO THEIRS. WE KNOCKED ON THE BACK DOOR AND WERE INVITED INTO THE KITCHEN BY MY GREAT GRANDMOTHER MARY AND THERE SAT AN OLD MAN WITH A LONG WHITE BEARD AT THE KITCHEN TABLE. IT WAS MY FIRST LOOK AT MY GREAT GRANDFATHER ELI. HE POINTED HIS FINGER AT ME AND ASKED, WHOSE BOY IS THIS?

GRANDMOTHER ELIZABETH REPLIED, THIS YOUNG GENTLEMAN IS RONALD, DARLENE AND RAYS SON.

BOTH OF THE GREAT GRANDPARENTS FACES LITE UP WITH BROAD SMILES AND SAID ALMOST IN UNISON, "DARLENES BOY"!! FOREVER AFTER THAT'S WHEN THEY TALKED TO ME, THEY CALLED ME BOY, AND WHENEVER THEY TALKED TO EACH OTHER THEY ALWAYS REFERRED TO ME AS DARLENES BOY. THEY NEVER USED MY FIRST NAME.

GRAMPA ELI MOTIONED FOR ME TO COME AND SIT AT THE TABLE WITH HIM AND ALMOST BY THE TIME THAT I GOT SAT DOWN, GRANDMOTHER MARY WAS PLACING A GLASS OF MILK AND A SMALL PLATE OF COOKIES IN FRONT OF ME. GRAMPA ELI WAS SITTING ACROSS THE TABLE FROM ME AND HE LOOKED AND TALKED RIGHT AT ME, ASKING ME QUESTIONS. ALTHOUGH I WAS USUALLY VERY SHY, I WAS ABLE TO TALK EASILY WITH HIM.

MY MOTHER WAS THE EIGHTH CHILD OF FOURTEEN AND THE SMALLEST. SHE WAS FOUR FOOT NINE AND WORE A SIZE THREE SHOE. I THINK HER TINY SIZE MAYBE MADE HER SPECIAL TO A LOT OF PEOPLE. EVERYBODY I EVER MET WHO KNEW HER, SEEMED TO LIKE HER.

THE NEXT MORNING I ASKED GRANDMOTHER ELIZABETH IF I COULD GO OVER AND VISIT WITH THE HUTCHINSONS. MAYBE I COULD HELP THEM WITH SOMETHING. GRANDMOTHER SAID THAT SHE THOUGHT IT WAS A FINE IDEA.

WHEN GRANDMOTHER MARY OPENED THE DOOR I ASKED HER STRAIGHT OUT IF THERE WAS SOMETHING THAT I COULD DO FOR HER. GRANDFATHER ELI SAID OVER HER SHOULDER, YOU CAN BRING SOME FIRE WOOD IN FOR THE KITCHEN STOVE. I'LL SHOW YOU WHERE IT IS. HE PUT ON A COAT AND CAP AND LED ME OUT TO THE GARAGE. HE OPENED THE WALK-IN DOOR AND WE WENT INTO THE GARAGE AND HE SHOWED ME WHERE HE KEPT THE WOOD.

HE EXPLAINED THAT WHEN HE BUILT THE GARAGE HE HAD MADE IT SIX FEET LONGER THEN HE NEEDED FOR THE CAR, IN THE FALL OF THE YEAR HE COULD STORE ENOUGH WOOD IN THE SPACE TO LAST ALL WINTER AND IT WOULD ALWAYS BE DRY. THE PIECES OF WOOD WERE CUT ONE FOOT LONG SO AS TO FIT IN THE COOKSTOVE IN THE KITCHEN AND THE FANCY POT-BELLIED STOVE IN THE PARLOR. IT TOOK ME FOUR TRIPS TO GET THE

STOVE WOOD IN AND THERE WAS MY PAY OF COOKIES AND MILK SITTING ON THE KITCHEN TABLE. GRAMPA SAT WITH ME. SIPPING A LARGE CUP OF COFFEE AND ASKING ME QUESTIONS.

ALMOST EVERY DAY EXCEPT SUNDAY I'D KNOCK ON THEIR KITCHEN DOOR, IT WAS LIKE I HAD A REGULAR JOB THERE AND THEY WERE EXPECTING ME. THEY'D ALWAYS HAVE SOMETHING FOR ME TO DO AND MY PAY WAS ALWAYS COOKIES AND MILK. BESIDES BRINGING IN THE STOVE WOOD GRANDMA MARY WOULD SEND ME ON SHORT ERRANDS, MOSTLY TO THE ROYAL BLUE STORE THAT WAS ABOUT A BLOCK FROM THEIR HOUSE. SHE WOULD GIVE ME A LIST OF THINGS SHE WANTED AND A CLOTH BAG TO CARRY THEM IN, IT NEVER WAS MUCH. I'D HAND THE LIST TO THE GROCER AND AS HE PUT THE ITEMS IN THE BAG HE'D WRITE THE PRICE ON THE LIST, WHEN HE HAD IT ALL IN THE BAG HE'D TOTAL IT UP AND GIVE THE LIST BACK TO ME AND SAY, I'LL ADD IT TO THEIR ACCOUNT. I NEVER HANDLED ANY MONEY. GRAMPA ELI SHOWED ME HOW TO PULL WEEDS IN THEIR VEGETABLE GARDEN OUT BACK AND GET THE ROOTS TOO. YOU PUT YOUR FINGERS RIGHT ON THE GROUND, TAKE AHOLD OF THE WEED AND WITH A STEADY SLOW PULL YOU'LL USUALLY GET THE ROOTS WITH THE WEEDS. HE TOOK AN OLD HOE AND SHORTENED THE HANDLE AND I HAD MY OWN HOE. HE SHOWED ME HOW TO LOOSEN THE DIRT AROUND GARDEN PLANTS WITH MY HOE WITHOUT HURTING THEM. HE WAS TEACHING ME TO BE A FARM BOY BY ME ACTUALLY DOING THE

HOUSE AND PUTTING THEM TOGETHER. WHEN I HAD FINISHED BUILDING THE BIRDHOUSE, I PAINTED IT WHITE WITH RED TRIM AND FASTENED IT HIGH UP ON THE GARAGE. THERE WERE A LOT OF LITTLE WRENS BORN IN THE HOUSE IN THE NEXT FEW YEARS. WHEN I WAS SIXTEEN, I BUILT A CANOE LIKE BOAT IN OUR ATTIC. THE FRONT OF THE BOAT AND THE BOAT WERE SHAPED LIKE A CANOE BUT I CUT THE BACK OF THE BOAT FLAT ACROSS SO A SMALL OUTBOARD MOTOR COULD BE USED ON IT. THE SHAPE OF THE BOAT WAS FINISHED AND I WANTED TO TAKE IT DOWN TO THE GARAGE AND PUT THE FINISHING TOUCHES ON IT. WHEN I TRIED TO TAKE IT DOWN THE STAIRS AND THROUGH THE HOUSE, I FOUND THAT THE HALLWAY AT THE BOTTOM OF THE STAIRS WAS TOO NARROW AND I COULDN'T TURN THE BOAT IN IT. THE ONLY WAY I COULD GET THE BOAT OUT OF THE HOUSE WAS THROUGH A DOUBLE WINDOW AT THE END OF THE ATTIC THAT WAS ABOVE THE BACK PORCH ROOF. I TOOK THE TWO WINDOWS COMPLETELY OUT, LOWERED THE BOAT ONTO THE PORCH ROOF, SECURED THE WINDOWS BACK IN PLACE, AND WATER-PROOFED THEM. THEN I TOOK THE BOAT OUT TO THE GARAGE AND FINISHED IT. DAD AND I ALWAYS WENT UP TO FOX LAKE FISHING IN THE SPRING, THAT'S WHEN THE FISHING WAS BEST THERE. I FASTENED A CAR-TOP RACK ON THE CAR AND DAD HELPED ME SECURE MY NEW BOAT TO IT AND WE DROVE UP TO THE LAKE. WE PUT THE BOAT IN THE WATER BUT DAD WOULDN'T GET INTO IT. I THINK HE WAS AFRAID THAT IT WOULD TURN OVER. I HAD BUILT A KEEL BOARD INTO THE BOTTOM

OF THE BOAT SO THAT IT WOULDN'T EASILY ROLL OVER. WE DIDN'T HAVE LIFE JACKETS AND DAD WAS A GOOD SWIMMER BUT HE WOULDN'T GET IN MY BOAT. HE WENT OVER TO THE BOATHOUSE AND RENTED A BOAT AND WE CAUGHT A NICE MESS OF FISH, SCALED AND CLEANED THEM AND PUT THEM ON ICE. THE NEXT MORNING AFTER BREAKFAST DAD COULDN'T WAIT TO GET DOWN TO THE DOCK AND OUT ON THE LAKE FOR MORE GOOD FISHING. WHEN HE STARTED TO PUT OUR EQUIPMENT INTO THE RENTED BOAT, I STOPPED HIM AND SAID, I HAVE TO TRY OUT MY NEW BOAT TODAY. AND I DID. WE FISHED TOGETHER THAT DAY, ONLY IN DIFFERENT BOATS AND WE BOTH ENJOYED THE FISHING TRIP.

I BUILT MANY THINGS THROUGH THE YEARS, MOSTLY SMALL THINGS THAT I GAVE TO MY MOTHER, MY GRANDMOTHERS AND SOME OF MY AUNTS AS GIFTS. SOME WERE TOWEL RACKS, NAPKIN HOLDERS, MAGAZINE RACKS AND OTHER SMALL HOUSEHOLD THINGS. MY MOTHER AND GRANDMOTHERS WERE THE BIGGEST INFLUENCE IN MY LIFE WHEN I WAS A LITTLE BOY. THEY TAUGHT ME MANNERS AND RESPECT FOR NOT ONLY LADIES AND OLDER PEOPLE, BUT FOR EVERYBODY AND FOR EVERY LIVING THING. EVERY PERSON IN THIS WORLD IS A HUMAN BEING AND HAS FEELINGS AND NOTHING IS GAINED BY HURTING ANYONE. YEARS LATER, I AND MY WIFE HAD TWO SMALL CHILDREN AND I WAS A YOUNG FIREMAN ON A RAILROAD, STRUGGLING TO MAKE HOUSE PAYMENTS, BUY LITTLE SHOES, FURNITURE AND ALL THE OTHER THINGS THAT YOUNG FAMILIES NEED.

A FRIEND OF MINE, ALSO A RAILROAD WORKER LIVED IN A VERY LARGE MOBILE PARK. THERE WERE ABOUT EIGHT HUNDRED MOBILES IN THE PARK. MY FRIEND BILL DECIDED TO BUILD A PORCH ON HIS MOBILE AND ASKED ME IF I'D HELP HIM.

THERE WAS NO HURRY; WE'D WORK ON THE PORCH WHEN WE HAD THE TIME. SOMETIMES WE'D WORK TOGETHER BUT MOST OF THE TIME WE WORKED ALONE.

WHILE WE WERE SLOWLY BUILDING THE PORCH SOME OF BILLS NEIGHBORS CAME AROUND TO SEE WHAT WE WERE DOING. WHEN WE WERE JUST ABOUT FINISHED WITH THE PORCH A FEW OF THEM ASKED IF WE WOULD BUILD THEM A PORCH. WE EXPLAINED TO THEM THAT WE WERE DOING IT IN OUR SPARE TIME, BUT IF THEY WEREN'T IN A BIG HURRY, WE'D DO IT FOR THEM. PRETTY SOON WE HAD A LIST OF CUSTOMERS. I'D FIND OUT WHAT KIND OF PORCH THEY WANTED AND DRAW UP THE PLANS GET THEM OK'ED AND WE WERE IN THE PORCH BUILDING BUSINESS. SOME OF THE PORCHES WERE JUST PLATFORMS WITH RAILINGS, SOME WERE WITH ROOFS AND A FEW WERE ENCLOSED. BILL AND I VENTURED INTO NEW TERRITORIES WITH EACH DIFFERENT SET OF PLANS.

IN LATE FALL WHEN WE WERE THROUGH BUILDING PORCHES FOR THE YEAR, BILLS WIFE HAD THEIR FIRST BABY. SOMETIME DURNG THE WINTER, BILL AND HIS WIFE DECIDED THAT THEY DIDN'T WANT TO RAISE THEIR

FAMILY IN A MOBILE PARK SO THEY SCRAPED TOGETHER THE DOWN PAYMENT AND BOUGHT A HOUSE OUT IN THE SUBURBS AND THAT KINDA CURTAILED OUR PORCH BUILDING BUSNESS. WE DID BUILD A FEW PORCHES THAT SUMMER BUT WE BOTH HAD A LOT OF THINGS THAT WE WANTED TO DO TO OUR OWN PLACES SO WE WENT OUT OF THE PORCH BUILDING BUSINESS FOR GOOD. WE DIDN'T KEEP TRACK OF HOW MANY PORCHES WE BUILT BUT WE BOTH FIGURED THAT IT WAS UPWARD OF FORTY. IT WAS A GOOD LEARNING EXPERIENCE AND THE EXTRA MONEY WE MADE, HELPED US BOTH A LOT.

I BUILT MORE PORCHES THROUGH THE YEARS, AND TOOLSHEDS AND DOG HOUSES AND PLAYHOUSES FOR CHILDREN AND ALSO FURNITURE, JUST A LOT OF THINGS. SOME PLACE THROUGH THE YEARS I CAME TO THE REALIZATION THAT IT ALL STARTED WITH THE BASICS THAT GRANDFATHER ELI HAD TAUGHT ME SO MANY YEARS AGO WHEN I WAS A LITTLE BOY. IT SEEMED THAT EVERY RURAL AND SMALL TOWN HOME THAT I WAS EVER IN BACK IN THE 1920S AND 30S HAD AN IRON, WOOD BURNING COOKSTOVE IN IT'S KITCHEN. ON A COLD DAY THAT WAS THE FIRST PLACE THAT A PERSON WOULD HEAD FOR WHEN THEY CAME INTO THE HOUSE. IF YOU WANTED MORE HEAT FROM THE STOVE, YOU COULD ADD SOME DRY CORN COBS TO THE FIRE. DRY CORN COBS BURN VERY HOT. GRANDFATHER ELI LOVED ROCKING CHAIRS, HE HAD TWO VERY BIG ROCKERS, AND ONE WAS IN THE PARLOR AND THE OTHER, ON THE FRONT PORCH. HE SPENT A GOOD DEAL OF HIS TIME IN ONE OR THE

OTHER OF THEM. SOMETIMES GRAMPA ELI WOULD SIT IN HIS ROCKER IN THE PARLOR, GENTLY ROCKING WITH HIS EYES CLOSED, AND I WOULD BE SITTING NEARBY IN A BIG BROWN LEATHER CHAIR, MAYBE LOOKING AT THE FUNNY PAPERS OR JUST RELAXING. NEITHER OF US SAYING A WORD FOR MINUTES AT A TIME. WE BOTH ENJOYED THOSE QUIET TIMES.

ONE AFTERNOON GRANMOTHER ELIZABETH TOLD ME THAT GRAMPA HUTCHINSON HAD BEEN A SOLDIER IN THE CIVIL WAR AND HAD BEEN IN PRESIDENT ABRAHAM LINCOLNS UNION ARMY.

I ASKED HER WHO PRESIDENT LINCOLN WAS AND SHE ANSWERED, WHY, HE WAS THE LEADER OF THIS WHOLE COUNTRY.

THE NEXT MORNING I ASKED GRANDFATHER ELI IF HE HAD EVER SEEN ABRAHAM LINCOLN?

GRANDFATHER SAT STRAIGHT UP IN HIS CHAIR, LOOKED AT ME AND STARTED TO CHUCKLE. WITH A WIDE SMILE ON HIS FACE HE ANSWERED, NO, I NEVER SAW MR. LINCOLN, BUT I FOUGHT FOR HIM. GRAMPA SEEMED TO THINK THAT THIS WAS QUITE A JOKE.

I DIDN'T KNOW ABOUT THE CIVIL WAR OR WHO MR. LINCOLN REALLY WAS, BUT I LAUGHED ALONG WITH GRAMPA ANYWAY.

ANOTHER TIME I ASKED GRAMPA ELI IF HE HAD ALWAYS HAD A BEARD? GRAMPA ELI HAD A FULL WHITE BEARD THAT HE KEPT NEATLY TRIMMED.

HE THOUGHT FOR A FEW MOMENTS AND THEN SAID, WELL, I WASN'T BORN WITH A BEARD.

WE BOTH LAUGHED AND LAUGHED. I WAS THINKING HOW FUNNY A LITTLE BABY WOULD LOOK WITH A BEARD. IT WAS ANOTHER JOKE THAT WE HAD JUST BETWEEN THE TWO OF US. HE THEN TOLD ME A STORY.

MANY, MANY YEARS BEFORE, WHEN HIS CHILDREN WERE SMALL, HE AND HIS WIFE MARY HAD SEVEN CHILDREN, SIX GIRLS AND A BOY. HE WENT ON; HE HAD DECIDED TO SHAVE OFF HIS BEARD. EARLY ONE MORNING, BEFORE THE CHILDREN WERE UP, HE DID SHAVE OFF HIS BEARD AND THEN WENT OFF TO WORK.

WHEN HE CAME HOME THAT EVENING AND ENTERED THE HOUSE, ALL OF THE CHILDREN STARTED SCREAMING AND CRYNG WHEN THEY SAW HIM, THEY WERE RUNNING THIS WAY AND THAT, LOOKING FOR PLACES TO HIDE. THEY THOUGHT THAT A STRANGER WAS INVADING THEIR HOME. NONE OF THEM HAD EVER SEEN THEIR FATHER WITHOUT A BEARD. WELL, GRAMPA LEFT THE HOUSE AND WENT TO THE FAR END OF THEIR PROPERTY AND STAYED THERE UNTIL THEIR MOTHER FINALLY WAS ABLE TO CONVINCE THE CHILDREN THAT

THE MAN WITHOUT THE BEARD WAS INDEED THEIR FATHER.

WHEN GRAMPA ELI WAS INVITED BACK INTO THE HOUSE THE CHILDREN STILL LOOKED AT HIM SUSPICIOUSLY, AND KEPT THEIR DISTANCE FROM HIM. HE STOOD IN THE MIDDLE OF THE ROOM AND MADE THEM ALL A PROMISE. HE WOULD GROW HIS BEARD BACK AND HE VOWED THAT HE WOULD NEVER SHAVE IT OFF AGAIN. HE WORE A BEARD FOR THE REST OF HIS LONG LIFE.

THERE WAS ONE TIME THAT I DIDN'T KNOW MY GRANDFATHER ELI. THE MINISTER OF OUR CHURCH HAD TO BE OUT OF TOWN FOR A WEEK AND HE ASKED GRANFATHER ELI IF HE WOULD GIVE THE SERMON ON THE NEXT SUNDAY, GRANDFATHER AGREED THAT HE WOULD.

NOW, I HAD ALWAYS KNOWN GRANDFATHER ELI AS A SOFT SPOKEN AND GENTLE MAN. I HAD NEVER HEARD HIM EVEN RAISE HIS VOICE. THIS WAS HOW I EXPECTED HIM TO GIVE THE SERMON. I WAS PROUD THAT HE WAS DOING IT. IT WOULD BE A REAL TREAT.

HE STARTED THE SERMON RIGHT OFF WITH RANTINGS AND RAVINGS IN A VERY HIGH PITCHED VOICE THAT I DIDN'T RECOGNIZE. SHOUTING ABOUT THE EVILS OF SIN. HE DIDN'T TALK ABOUT THE LOVE OF GOD OR JESUS. IT WAS ALL ABOUT SIN. HE WENT ON AND ON, WAVING

HIS ARMS AROUND AND POINTING AT THE PEOPLE IN THE CHURCH. I THOUGHT THAT HE'D NEVER STOP.

THAT WASN'T MY GRANDFATHER UP THERE TALKING, IT WAS JOHN BROWN, THE ABOLITIONISH, WITH WILD EYES AND FLOWING BEARD. I DIDN'T KNOW THIS MAN IN THE PULPIT. NOR DID I WANT TO KNOW HIM. HE FRIGHTENED ME.

THE TWO GRANDMOTHERS HAD PLANNED AN OUTING FOR THAT AFTERNOON. WE'D DRIVE OVER TO ROCK CREEK, HAVE A PICNIC LUNCH AND RELAX IN THE COOLNESS UNDER THE TREES, AT THE DUDLEY SCHOOLHOUSE, AFTER LUNCH.

AFTER THE CHURCH SERVICES WERE OVER, WE WALKED THE HALF BLOCK TO THE HUTCHINSON HOME. GRAMPA ELI AND I CHANGED OUR CLOTHES WHILE THE LADIES WERE BUSY PREPARING THE LUNCH.

MY OTHER GRAMPA, HUMPHREY COULDN'T JOIN US, HE WAS THE ASSISTANT STATION MASTER FOR THE RAILROAD AND WORKED WEEKENDS. GRAMPA ELI AND I GOT HIS CAR OUT OF THE GARAGE AND HE SHOWED ME SOME THINGS ABOUT THE CAR. IT WAS A MODEL-T FORD AND HAD ONLY ONE DOOR IN THE FRONT; IT WAS ON THE DRIVES SIDE. GRAMPA OPENED THE DOOR AND SHOWED ME HOW THE SEAT FOLDED UP FORWARD AND UNDER THAT SEAT WAS THE GAS TANK. THERE WAS AN OPENING BETWEEN THE TWO FRONT SEATS SO THAT

YOU COULD WALK INTO THE BACK SEAT AREA. THE PASSENGER SEAT ALSO FOLDED FORWARD. THERE WAS ONLY ONE DOOR TO THE BACK SEAT AND IT WAS ON THE PASSENGER SIDE, A LITTLE BACK FROM THE MIDDLE OF THE CAR. THE MODEL-T FORD WAS A HIGH WHEELED CAR, SO THERE WAS A STEP TO HELP YOU CLIMB INTO THE BACK SEAT. THE CAR KINDA REMINDED ME OF THE STAGE COACHES THAT I HAD SEEN IN THE WESTERN MOVIES.

GRAMPA ELI SLOWLY DROVE OUT OF TOWN WITH ME IN THE OTHER FRONT SEAT. THE LADIES SAT IN THE BACK. GRAMPA HAD TOLD ME THAT GRANDMOTHER MARY NEVER RODE IN THE FRONT SEAT EVEN WHEN IT WAS ONLY THE TWO OF THEM IN THE CAR.

AS SOON AS WE REACHED THE CITY LIMITS, GRAMPA STEPPED ON THE GAS. I HEARD GRANMOTHER MARY SAY, IN A HIGH PITHCED VOICE, FOR HIM TO SLOW DOWN. I GUESS THAT HE GOT KINDA DEAF WHEN HE WAS DRIVING THE CAR BECAUSE HE DIDN'T RESPOND TO HER AT ALL. HE LOOKED STRAIGHT AHEAD AND I NOTICED A SMALL SMILE ON HIS FACE. I THINK HE ENJOYED GOING A LITTLE FAST.

WHEN WE GOT TO ROCK CREEK WE TURNED INTO THE PARKING LOT OF A SMALL, FRESHLY PAINTED SCHOOLHOUSE THAT SAT RIGHT IN THE CENTER OF THE YARD. THE PLACE WAS WELL CARED FOR WITH SWINGS. A SLIDE AND TEETER-TOTTERS IN THE PLAYGROUND AREA

AND THERE WAS A LARGE TREE TO ONE SIDE WITH TWO PICNIC TABLES UNDER IT. THE ENTIRE SCHOOL AREA WAS CLOSED IN WITH AN IRON PIPE FENCE. THERE WERE VARIOUS KINDS OF FLOWERS ALONG THE FENCE LINE AND AROUND THE SCHOOL. OUR TWO LADIES WALKED ALONG THE FENCE DISCUSSING THE FLOWERS.

GRAMPA AND I SAT AT ONE OF THE PICNIC TABLES AND HE TOLD ME A STORY. AFTER THE WAR HE WENT BACK TO BEING A CARPENTER AND BUILDING THIS SCHOOL WAS ONE OF THE FIRST JOBS THAT HE TOOK ON. IT WASN'T A REALLY BIG JOB AND HE COULD HONE UP HIS CARPENTRY SKILLS THAT HAD BEEN PUT ASIDE FOR THE LAST THREE YEARS BECAUSE OF THE WAR, HE'D TAKE HIS TIME. HE HAD ALL SUMMER.

AFTER THE FOUNDATION WAS IN PLACE, HE, ALONG WITH TWO HELPERS COMMENCED TO LAY DOWN THE FLOOR. JUST BEFORE NOON A HANDSOME YOUNG LADY APPEARED, SHE SAT DOWN ON THAT VERY LARGE ROCK OVER THERE, HE POINTED AT THE ROCK. SHE SEEMED TO BE VERY INTRESTED IN WHAT WE WERE DOING. SHORTLY WE STOPPED FOR LUNCH AND I WENT OVER TO WHERE SHE WAS SITTING, INTRODUCED MYSELF AND OFFERED HER ONE OF MY SNADWICHES. SHE ACCEPTED THE SANDWICH AND SAID THAT HER NAME WAS MARY DUDLEY AND SHE WAS GOING TO BE THE TEACHER HERE AT THE SCHOOL IN THE FALL. I KEPT TALKING TO HER. ACTUALLY, I WAS SO TAKEN BY HER THAT I COULD HARDLY BREATH.

THE NEXT DAY SHE CAME AGAIN AT ABOUT THE SAME TIME. THIS TIME SHE BROUGHT ALONG A FRESHLY BAKED APPLE PIE. MY HELPERS ENJOYED EATING ABOUT HALF OF IT. IT WAS DELICIOUS.

I PUT MY HELPERS BACK TO WORK AND TALKED TO HER MUCH LONGER THAN I SHOULD HAVE. I WAS STALLING, TRYING TO WORK UP THE NERVE TO ASK HER TO A BARN DANCE THAT WAS BEING HELD OUT AT FRANK BROWNS FARM THE COMING SATURDAY. I FINALLY GOT AROUND TO ASKING HER AND SHE ACCEPTED MY INVITATION.

WE WENT TO THE DANCE AND SHE DIDN'T SEEM TO NOTICE HOW CLUMSY I WAS. I FLOATED ON A CLOUD THAT NIGHT AND IT'S BEEN THAT WAY EVER SINCE. FROM THAT NIGHT ON, WE'VE BEEN LIKE TWO PEAS IN A POD AND IT ALL STARTED RIGHT HERE. MARY WAS MY ONE AND ONLY SWEETHEART, THE ONLY ONE I EVER WANTED. WE WERE MARRIED THAT YEAR AND SHE'S STILL MY SWEETHEART, AFTER ALMOST SEVENTY YEARS. GRAMPA TOLD ME ON THE WAY HOME THAT WE WERE GOING FISHING IN THE MORNING, AND HE ADDED. COME OVER HERE EARLY. THE FISH IN MY SECRET FISHING SPOT WILL BE WAITING FOR THEIR BREAKFAST. WHEN I GOT TO GRAMPAS HOUSE THE NEXT MORNING, GRAMP WAS EATING A BIG BOWL OF OATMEAL. GRANDMOTHER MARY SET OUT MY MILK AND COOKIES AND ASKED GRAMPA IF SHE SHOULD MAKE SOME SANDWICHES. HE ANSWERED NO; THE FISH WON'T BITE WHEN THE SUN'S HIGH AND THE DAY WARMS UP. WE'LL BE HOME BY LUNCHTIME.

AFTER WE WERE THROUGH EATING, WE WENT OUT AND GOT THE CAR OUT OF THE GARAGE. GRAMPA WENT BACK IN AND CAME BACK CARRYING A CIGAR BOX AND A SMALL PAIL. THE BOX HELD HOOKS, SINKERS, BOBBERS AND SOME HEAVY STRING. THE PAIL WAS HALF FULL OF DIRT AND WHAT HE CALLED, HIS OWN SPECIAL BAIT. I ASKED HIM WHAT BAIT WAS. THIS WAS THE FIRST TIME THAT I HAD EVER BEEN FISHING.

HE ANSWERED, RED SQUIGGLEY, LIVELY ANGLE WORMS FROM THE HUTCHINSON GARDEN. FISH JUST LOVE MY SPECIAL WORMS.

WHEN WE GOT TO THE RIVER GRAMPA SAID, NOW BOY, I'VE NEVER TAKEN ANYBODY TO MY SECRET FISHING SPOT BEFORE; WE'VE GOT TO KEEP THIS PLACE A SECRET JUST BETWEEN THE TWO OF US. WE DON'T WANT HALF THE TOWNSHIP COMING DOWN HERE AND CATCHING ALL THE FISH IN THE RIVER. DO WE? I SHOOK MY HEAD AND SAID, NO. GRAMPA HAD TIED TWO CANE POLES TO THE SIDE OF THE CAR, HE CARRIED THEM AND I BROUGHT ALONG THE BOX AND PAIL OF WORMS. WE WALKED DOWN A PATH FOR A WAYS AND GRAMPA SAID OVER HIS SHOULDER, WE'RE ALMOST THERE. HE STOPPED SUDDENLY. THERE WERE TWO LADIES WEARING BIG HATS, SITTING ON FOLD-UP CHAIRS AND THEY WERE FISHING.

WE WALKED UP TO THEM AND GRAMPA SAID, GOOD MORNING LADIES, HOW'S THE FISHING THIS MORNING?

THEY BOTH SAID HELLO, AND ONE OF THEM SAID, FISHING'S VERY GOOD SO FAR.

WE WALKED ON DOWN THE PATH A WAYS AND GRAMPA SAID, I GUESS THIS'LL DO. WE STOPPED AND STARTED GETTING READY TO FISH. I ASKED IF THIS WAS HIS SECRET SPOT.

HE SAID NO, THE WHITE SISTERS ARE IN OUR SPOT. GRAMPA RIGGED UP OUR POLES, BAITED THE HOOKS AND SHOWED ME HOW TO FISH. WE SAT ON A LOG AND FISHED UNTIL THE DAY STARTED TO GET HOT, THEN GRAMPA SAID, IT MUST BE COMING ONTO LUNCH TIME, LET'S GO HOME AND GET SOME VITTLES.

WE HAD ONLY CAUGHT FOUR LITTLE SUNFISH; I CAUGHT ONE, MY FIRST CATCH EVER. WE PUT THEM BACK IN THE RIVER AND GRAMPA TOLD THEM TO GROW UP AND WE'D SEE THEM LATER.

ON THE WAY HOME GRAMPA SAID, I WONDER HOW THOSE LADIES KNEW WHERE OUR SECRET SPOT WAS. NOW IT WAS OUR SPOT, WHICH KINDA PUFFED ME UP A BIT. HE WENT ON; MAYBE THEY'VE BEEN SPYING ON ME.

GRAMDFATHER ELI AND I FISHED MANY TIMES THROUGH THE YEARS WITH MUCH SUCCESS, MOST TIMES AT OUR SECRET SPOT. WE DIDN'T TALK A LOT, IT WASN'T NECESSARY. JUST BEING THERE NEXT TO THE

GUIET RIVER, IN THE COOLNESS UNDER THE TREES WAS ENOUGH FOR BOTH GRAMPA AND ME.

THE YEAR WAS 1936 WHEN MY FAMILY RECEIVED THE ANNOUNCEMENT THAT THERE WAS GOING TO BE A CELEBRATION IN NORA SPRINGS. GRANDMOTHER AND GRANDFATHER HUTCHINSON WERE HAVING THEIR SEVENTIETH WEDDING ANNIVERSARY AND ANYONE RELATED TO THEM SHOULD TRY TO ATTEND THE CELEBRATION. THE GET TOGETHER WOULD BE HELD IN THE FORM OF A PICNIC IN OLD SETTLER PARK IN NORA SPRINGS, IOWA.

MY FAMILY, THE GIFFORDS MADE SURE WE WERE THERE. IT WAS A VERY SPECIAL OCCASION FOR ME, BOTH MARY AND ELI WERE SO DEAR TO ME. I MET PEOPLE THAT I HAD NEVER SEEN OR EVEN HEARD OF BEFORE. I KNEW THAT I HAD A LOT OF AUNTS AND UNCLES, BUT WHERE DID ALL THE COUSINS COME FROM? THERE WERE MOBS OF CHILDREN EVERYWHERE. I MET MANY, MANY NICE PEOPLE THAT DAY, A LOT OF WHO I NEVER SAW AGAIN. SOME BOYS AND I CLIMBED UP ON OLD SETTLE, THE BIG ROCK THAT THE PARK WAS NAMED FOR. WHEN I STOOD UP AND LOOKED AROUND, I COULD SEE THAT THE PARK WAS FULL TO OVER FLOWING WITH ALL SIZES AND AGES OF DECENDENTS OF MARY AND ELI HUTCHINSON. IT WAS A GREAT DAY FOR THEM AND EVERYONE. SADLY, THE FOLLOWING YEAR DEAR, SWEET GIVING GREAT GRANDMOTHER MARY PASSED AWAY. SHE WAS 93 AND GRAMPA ELI WAS 99. THEY HAD BEEN MARRIED FOR

SEVENTY ONE YEARS AND HAD SPENT ALL BUT TWO OF THOSE YEARS IN NORA SPRINGS. IN 1871 AND 72 THEY HOMESTEADED IN MINNESOTA BUT DECIDED THAT NORA SPRINGS, IOWA WAS WHERE THEY REALLY WANTED TO LIVE AND THEY MOVED BACK.

THE HEADLINES OF THE NORA SPSRINGS ADVERTISER, DATED JUNE 1ST 1939 READ, ELI HUTCHINSON TO BE 101 YEARS OLD NEXT WEDNESDAY. THERE WAS A PICTURE OF GRAMPA AND UNDER IT, IT SAID, NORA SPRINGS OLDEST LIVING CITIZEN AND LAST CIVIL WAR VETERAN.

I REGRET THAT I WAS UNABLE TO BE THERE FOR GRAMPA ELIS BIRTHDAY. WE DID GO TO IOWA FOR A FEW DAYS IN JULY. GRANDMOTHER ELIZABETH AND GRANDFATHER HUMPHREY HAD MOVED IN WITH GRAMPA ELI, SO AS TO TAKE CARE OF HIM.

WHEN MY DAD PULLED OUR CAR UP IN FRONT OF GRAMPAS HOUSE, MY GRANDPARENTS CAME OUT TO GREET US. WHEN THE GREETINGS WERE OVER I SAID TO GRANDMOTHER ELIZABETH THAT I'D LIKE TO SEE GRAMPA ELI. SHE QUICKLY SAID YES, GO RIGHT IN. I KNOW HE'LL BE HAPPY TO SEE YOU. HE'S IN THE PARLOR SITTING IN HIS ROCKER. HE MAY NOT KNOW YOU RIGHT AWAY; HIS EYES HAVE GROWN VERY WEAK. TELL HIM WHO YOU ARE AND SIT WITH HIM FOR A WHILE. I KNOW HE'LL ENJOY THAT.

I OPENED THE FRONT DOOR AND WALKED DOWN THE HALL TO THE PARLOR THAT I HAD SO MANY TIMES THROUGH THE YEARS SAT IN WITH MY GREAT GRANDFATHER. I WENT INTO THE PARLOR AND THERE SAT GRAMPA ELI. HE WAS KINDA BENT OVER IN HIS BIG ROCKING CHAIR, WITH HIS CHIN RESTING ON HIS CHEST.

I WALKED OVER TO HIM AND GENTLY TOOK AHOLD OF HIM BY HIS SHOULDERS AND STRAIGHTENED HIM UP IN HIS CHAIR. HE SHOOK HIMSELF A LITTLE AND BLINKED HIS EYES OPEN. BY THIS TIME I WAS STANDING DIRECTLY IN FRONT OF HIM. HE BLINKED HIS EYES AGAIN, LOOKED AT ME AND WITH A HINT OF A SMILE ON HIS WIDE MOUTH HE SAID, IN A HOARSE WHISPER, DARLENES BOY.

IT WASN'T A QUESTION, HE KNW WHO I WAS.

I SAID, YES GRANFATHER, IT'S ME.

THOSE WERE THE LAST WORDS THAT WE EVER SPOKE TO EACH OTHER. HE LIFTED HIS LEFT HAND A LITTLE AND I TOOK IT IN BOTH MY HANDS. I FELT A FAINT SQUEEZE OF HIS HAND AND THEN IT RELAXED. I HELD ONTO HIS HAND FOR A SHORT MINUTE AND THEN LAYED IT ON THE ARMREST OF HIS CHAIR. HE PUT HIS HEAD BACK AGAINST THE HEADREST OF HIS CHAIR, SIGHED, CLOSED HIS EYES AND SLOWLY BEGAN TO ROCK. IN TWO OR THREE MINUTES THE ROCKING STOPPED, HE WAS ASLEEP. I WENT ACROSS THE ROOM AND SAT IN THE BIG

BROWN LEATHER CHAIR AND LEANED BACK. GRAMPA ELI AND I SHARED ANOTHER QUIET HOUR TOGETHER, HE NEVER STIRRED.

MY GREAT GRANDFATHER HUTCHINSON DIED LATER THAT YEAR AND MY FAMILY ATTENDED THE FUNERAL. THOUGH THERE WERE MASSES OF PEOPLE AT THE CHURCH AND THE CEMENTRY, I FELT ABSOLUTELY ALONE, WITH A GREAT FEELING OF EMPTINESS.

IT WASN'T ONLY THE THINGS THAT HE HAD TAUGHT ME ABOUT FISHING, CARPENTRY, GARDENING AND OTHER THINGS. THERE WERE ALSO THE UNSPOKEN THINGS THAT I LEARNED, JUST BEING WITH HIM FOR WHAT SEEMS LIKE A VERY SHORT ELEVEN YEARS, THAT HAVE STUCK WITH ME AND SERVED ME EVER AFTER. WE WERE PALS, COMPANIONS, AND FRIENDS. THANK YOU SIR. REST IN PEACE GRANDFATHER...... DARLENES BOY......